David

Best of Life

[illegible]

How Ordinary People Become Millionaires

HOW ORDINARY PEOPLE BECOME MILLIONAIRES

AN INVESTMENT STRATEGY THAT PROFITS FROM TAX REFORM

Louis F. Petrossi

VANTAGE PRESS
New York / Washington / Atlanta
Los Angeles / Chicago

This publication is designed to provide accurate and authoritative information, not legal advice. Events and laws may change after publication. The author and publisher specifically disclaim any liability, loss, or risk—personal or otherwise—which is incurred as a consequence, directly or indirectly, of the use and application of any of the contents of the work. Before acting on any suggestion presented in the book, legal or other professional assistance may be advisable.

FIRST EDITION

Published by Vantage Press, Inc.
516 West 34th Street, New York, New York 10001

Manufactured in the United States of America
ISBN: 0-533-07023-6

Library of Congress Catalog Card No.: 86-90056

To my loving wife Stephanie and four children:
Tiffany, Mary Beth, Susan, and Louis, Jr.

You are and become what you think you are.

CONTENTS

INTRODUCTION

Aristotle, the ancient Greek philosopher, once said, "All men naturally desire to know." Today, in the modern age of the entrepreneur, most people naturally desire to know how financial planning is making working people millionaires.

GUIDE YOUR OWN DESTINY

Many people in our society feel that we live in a world economy so complex and so full of problems that the chances of becoming a millionaire are slim to none. They cite high taxes, government deficits, never-ending inflation, bad luck, lack of time, limited investment knowledge, and hundreds of other seemingly logical reasons to justify their financial disappointment. Other people share an entrepreneurial spirit. These people have made both good and terribly bad investments. However, they are extremely grateful and cherish the opportunity to live in a democracy that gives all people the freedom of choice. They refuse to place their fate in the hands of their employers. Every one of them believes and knows that numerous opportunities are available in the United States to build and to keep massive wealth. Our nation offers every form of potential riches in great abundance.

THE PURPOSE OF THIS BOOK

It is necessary to bridge the psychological and financial obstacles that prevent people from becoming millionaires with a blueprint and plan of action for success. It is a game plan that working people on fixed salaries can understand, believe, implement, and even modify, based on changing personal situations and available resources. It is a financial plan that even allows working people to start the quest to become a millionaire on a part-time basis. You can decide to be a passive investor. You can be a dynamic, active investor. You can start with no money, some of your money, or all of your money. You can acquire a million dollars over a life span or several life spans or decide to expedite the process in a few years.

One common trait of all millionaires is that they invest their money wisely. Millionaires also possess competitive advantages that appear in the forms of knowledge, skills, and attitude. This book provides a diversified plan of action and reveals several trade secrets that have helped hundreds and thousands of different people become millionaires. You can use some of these trade secrets now and others when the right time comes. Which trade secret will work best for you? It all depends on your personal resources, motivation, risk tolerance, energy level, goals, and time period in which you wish to acquire a million dollars. You will soon learn several proven methods to accomplish your financial desires.

WHAT TO EXPECT FROM THIS BOOK

1. It will show you how to become a millionaire without changing your job (like it or not) or present salary.
2. It will explain the effective ways for you to get started now with little or no money.
3. It will crystallize new ways for you to increase your cash flow and net worth.
4. It will show you how and where to make a lot of money on small investments.
5. It will introduce you to the 70–20–10 investment strategy for the coming decade.
6. It will outline ways for you to select and analyze the investments that fit your personal situation.

7. It will show you where to find the outstanding real-estate and stock-market investments.
8. It will show you how and where to prosper as a passive investor.
9. It will help you to negotiate more efficiently for the things you need.
10. It will show you how to diversify your investment portfolio.
11. It will explain how to track and monitor your goals and success.
12. It will detail how to do more with your time and money (leverage).
13. It will show you how to reduce the investment risk.
14. It will explain how you can save immense time working with experts.
15. It will show you how to eliminate stress, which causes unhappiness, strokes, and death.
16. It will provide case studies and formulas to help you see the opportunities at your fingertips.
17. It will develop a flexible approach for your long-term financial planning, namely The Ten Commandments of Wealth.
19. It will encourage you to share your new knowledge and help other deserving people improve their financial situation.
20. It will give you peace of mind and a deep feeling of pride and dignity that comes when you control your own destiny.
21. It will serve as a reference source you can use for the rest of your life.

Take a deep breath and slowly exhale all your doubts and fears. Your desires and plans for the future are within your reach. Now is the time to decide that you are becoming a new millionaire. Close your eyes and think of your million-dollar estate. Now, take another deep breath and slowly exhale the misfortunes you have experienced in the past. Now enjoy reading chapter 1: "The Million-Dollar Numbers Game."

Part I

HOW TO POSITION YOURSELF FOR FINANCIAL SUCCESS

Chapter 1

THE MILLION-DOLLAR NUMBERS GAME

Most millionaires in the United States started with little or no money to build a financial empire. These people had great hopes and expectations. They were resourceful and determined to build a fortune with limited capital. They desired riches.

WHAT IS CAPITAL?

The *American Heritage Dictionary of the English Language* defines capital as "wealth in the form of money or property . . . any asset or advantage." Later, we will discuss several assets and advantages that are available for you to build wealth, in addition to the hard cash in your money market, bank savings, and checking accounts.

START INVESTING NOW

Why is it so important to start investing now? The answer is in the compounding effect of monies (interest on interest) plus capital gains profits invested over a period of time. Why is it equally important for you to select the investments with the best profit and yield compatible with your risk tolerance? There are two major benefits. First, a higher profit yield will allow you to reach your goal of one million dollars with *less* money invested. Secondly, and of greater value, by investing the same amount of capital and getting the higher profit yield, you will be able to accumulate much more than a million dollars over the same investment period. Let's analyze a lump sum, one-time, fixed dollar investment, and a periodic monthly investment. The profit yields will be at 10 percent and 15 percent, and the growth of the dollar amount invested will be determined by the length of the holding period or time for the investment. You will quickly see how higher profit yields, of only a few percentage points, make a tremendous profit difference even in time-deposit investment accounts.

LUMP SUM, ONE-TIME DOLLAR INVESTMENT

Chart number 1 shows the lump sum, one-time dollar investment necessary for people of different ages to acquire one million dollars by age sixty-five. The dollar amounts invested are compounded annually, both with a 10-percent and a 15-percent profit yield. The younger or earlier a person starts, the lesser the dollar amount required to accumulate a million dollars. The majority of millionaires acquired their fortunes between the ages of forty and sixty. Why? These people waited that many years to decide and believe they could accomplish that goal and purpose. Chart 1 merely shows that you can make that decision at any age, regardless of where you work or what your salary is.

Chart 1
One-time, Lump Sum Investment

Age	Dollar Investment 10% Profit Yield	15% Profit Yield	Time Period For $1,000,000
25	$ 22,094	$ 3,733	40 years
30	$ 35,584	$ 7,508	35 years
35	$ 57,308	$ 15,103	30 years
40	$ 92,296	$ 30,377	25 years
45	$148,644	$ 61,100	20 years
50	$239,392	$122,894	15 years
55	$385,543	$247,185	10 years
60	$620,921	$497,177	5 years

Let's analyze the 25-year-old person. The 15-percent profit yield requires an investment of $3,733, which is almost six times LESS than the $22,094 necessary for a 10-percent profit yield to grow to $1,000,000 over a 40-year time period. The purpose of the numbers game is to show you how to use time. The chapters on investments will show you where to find the profit yields and investments for your personal situation.

Trade Secret Number 1

The sooner you start investing and reinvesting your profits, the more wealth you will earn.

Trade Secret Number 2

Be patient and give your investment sufficient time to harvest wealth.

The same 25-year-old person who has $22,094 invested at a 15-percent profit yield, instead of the 10-percent profit yield, will accumulate $5,918,177 over the same 40-year period. A small 5-percent difference in the profit yield from 10 percent to 15 percent equals $4,918,177 more wealth.

Trade Secret Number 3

It pays huge dividends to shop around for the best profit-yields.

On chart 1, the 40-year-old person yielding 15 percent needs to invest $30,377, which is more than three times less than the $92,296 necessary for the 10-percent profit yield to grow to $1,000,000 over a 25-year time span. Let's suppose the 40-year-old person has $92,296 in money market or time-deposit accounts yielding 10 percent and now finds a 15-percent profit yield after reading Trade Secret Number 4. The $92,296 will now be able to grow to $3,038,287, instead of $1,000,000, over the same 25-year time period. It really pays for all working people to continue to live on salary paychecks and to continue to reinvest all the profits on their investments.

Trade Secret Number 4

Reinvest every penny of your investment profits until you reach your dollar goal.

PERIODIC MONTHLY INVESTMENTS

In today's age of consumption, with mass advertising competing for all the monies you earn, plus your fondest desires to live the good life, most working people do not have the lump sum monies available for immediate investment purposes. Working people are very comfortable budgeting monthly dollar amounts for rent, mortgage, food, auto, clothes, and so on. Keeping in mind that spending is a well-established habit, let's analyze the periodic monthly investments necessary to accumulate $1,000,000 by age 65. In chart 2 we will use the same 10-percent and 15-percent profit yields compounded monthly.

Chart 2
Monthly
Dollar Investment

Age	10% Profit Yield	15% Profit Yield	$1,000,000 At Age 65
25	$ 156.82	$ 31.85	
30	261.22	67.29	
35	438.73	142.66	
40	747.45	304.50	
45	1,306.99	659.65	
50	2,392.00	1,477.40	
55	4,841.40	3,588.64	
60	12,806.99	11,150.55	

Chart 2 shows that the 25-year-old person who selects a 15-percent profit yield can become a millionaire by salting away only $1.06 per day for investment purposes. You will agree that $1.06 per day saved for investment purposes will put a small dent in most 25-year-old wage-earners' budgets. The same 25-year-old working person would need to save only $5.23 per day with the 10-percent profit yield. Chart 2 shows that the 40-year-old wage-earner who chooses a 15-percent profit yield needs to save only $10.15 per day to accumulate $1,000,000 over a 25-year time period.

Review chart 1 and chart 2, and start thinking about one-time, lump sum dollar, and/or periodic monthly dollar amounts you can invest to start building your wealth.

Trade Secret Number 5

Comfortable monthly investments build massive wealth over a period of time.

Trade Secret Number 6

Perseverance and time are both noncash assets that create all millionaires.

Trade Secret Number 7

A new wave of part-time workers and investors are quietly becoming millionaires.

THE RULE OF 72

You are probably wondering what kind of computer or calculator I need to crunch the numbers and to figure out my investment profits? Later in this book, many formulas, case studies, and equations will be simply stated to allow you to quickly figure out the bottom-line profit return on your investments.

"The Rule of 72" is a formula you can start using immediately. Get a scratch pad and a pencil, and we'll start putting this formula to work for your practical use. It only takes a few seconds to learn, so get your paper and pencil ready.

The Rule of 72 is a quick method for you to figure out how long it will take to double your money, given an annual percent profit yield. The Rule of 72 is based on the fact that it takes 72 years for a one-percent (1%) profit yield to double in value. For instance, $100 compounded at one percent will double in value to $200 in 72 years.

Rule of 72 Formula

Seventy-two divided by percent yield equals the time it takes to double your money.

72 ÷ % yield = Number of years it takes to double your money

Let's assume you can get a 6-percent, 8-percent, 10-percent, and 15-percent return on different investments and you now want to know how long it will take you to double your money.

The 6-percent return is in a savings account and the dollar

amount is $1,000. How long will it take to double your money to $2,000?

Answer:

72 ÷ 6 = 12 years, for $1,000 to grow to $2,000 with a 6-percent growth compounded annually.

Your $100,000 home is going up in value at 8 percent per year. How many years will it take to double in value to $200,000?

Answer:

72 ÷ 8 = 9 years, for $100,000 to grow to $200,000 with an 8-percent annual-compounded appreciation.

Trade Secret Number 8

Most hard assets, such as real estate, double in value at least every nine years.

The 10-percent profit yield is in a certificate of deposit. How long will it take the $1,000 to grow in value to $2,000?

Answer:

72 ÷ 10 = 7.2 years to double your money.

What about a 15-percent profit yield?

Answer:

72 ÷ 15 = 4.8 years to double your money.

The Rule of 72 will now be helpful to you, with interest-bearing accounts, and very exciting and profitable when we discuss "LEVERAGED" real-estate investments in a later chapter. Read the next sentence twice. Once you control a fixed dollar amount of investment assets and you determine the annual rate of growth, it will be easy to figure out the number of years it takes for your assets to double in value *and* grow to a million dollars.

THE MILLION-DOLLAR NUMBERS GAME RAISES MANY ISSUES

The numbers game raises many good questions. Some are answered in chapter 2, others throughout the book. One popular question you might be asking is, "Sure, I'm going to become a millionaire; but what will a million dollars be worth several years later, taking inflation into consideration?" That's an excellent and fair question that we explore in depth throughout this book. For now, just remember that our major purpose here is to bridge the psychological and financial obstacles that prevent people from becoming millionaires by giving you a blueprint and plan of action that makes both the quest and monetary reward worthwhile.

The million-dollar numbers game is a source of encouragement and proof that you do possess the money, assets, property, resources, and advantages to become a millionaire in your life span, or combined over a partner's life span, or within a few years or perhaps even a few months. It may take you thirty long years instead of thirty short months. Regardless of when you achieve it, let's focus on the future value of one million dollars.

UNDERSTAND INFLATION

Inflation eats away and destroys the future buying power of the U.S. dollar. Since World War II, every year has been inflationary except 1949 and 1955. All economists and government officials talk about "controlling" inflation. Nobody talks about "eliminating" inflation. You can expect inflation to range from 3 percent to 20 percent over the next twenty years. Plan on inflation, and learn how to profit from inflation.

FUTURE VALUE OF ONE MILLION DOLLARS

No way is a million dollars today worth what it was thirty years ago. Your mind is capable of doing amazing things. Think back thirty years in time to the known past. Food, clothing, energy, real estate, and transportation all cost much less thirty years ago. At this time, as you are reading, in the only free democracy in the world, less than one-half of one percent of the people living in the United States are millionaires. Thirty long years ago, 99.5 percent of the working people had the same feelings and concerns about the future value of one million dollars. I agree that money is not a storage of value and that inflation will diminish future purchasing power. However, I have met few people who would walk away from a million dollars or the opportunity to enhance their present financial position.

Trade Secret Number 9

The opinions and advice of nonmillionaires may guide you to poverty.

Trade Secret Number 10

More money will always serve your future needs better than less money.

Nevertheless, thirty years from today, one million dollars will not buy the goods and services that it can now. If inflation averages 6 percent, a conservative projection for the next thirty years, the buying power of one million dollars will decrease to $174,100. Don't be alarmed, because there are several beneficial ways to hedge against inflation. The chart 1 lump sum dollar investment for a 35-year-old person to acquire a million dollars is $15,103 with a 15-percent profit yield over a 30-year period. If we discount the $15,103 by the 6-percent inflation factor, the future value of the $15,103 is $2,629.59. Which is better: $174,100 or $2,629.59? The later chapters reveal investment vehicles that will allow you to counter inflation and offset the rising costs of goods and services. Your salary increases will barely keep up with inflation throughout your work career. The major issue to ponder and figure out is, "How much money will I need to maintain my life-style and purchase goods and services during the nonworking retirement years?"

Trade Secret Number 11

Money is only a storage of value when it is invested above the rate of inflation.

STAY ON TRACK

The person who decides to acquire a million dollars or more, subject to inflation, will still have many advantages over the people who decided it wasn't in their best interest to create a million-dollar estate. Looking at inflation from another point of view, a modest net worth estate today will become a super-inadequate estate in 30 years, due to never-ending inflation.

The chapters in the book devoted to "leverage" and real-estate investments will show you how to overcome the negative aspects of inflation and how to build inflation-indexed wealth for the years ahead.

Trade Secret Number 12

The rich always strive to get richer in order to preserve and increase the value of their money.

The "Numbers Game" is important in all investment decisions that you will make. Your overall success is dependent on long-term, diversified investment opportunities that build wealth and outpace inflation. Hopefully, you have decided that it is in your best interest to become a millionaire. You might even be planning to accumulate several million dollars over your life span.

The foundation on which to build your wealth and success is explained in the next chapter, "The Most Important Noncash Investment You Can Make."

Trade Secret Number 13

Success only comes to those people who become success conscious.

Chapter 2

THE MOST IMPORTANT NONCASH INVESTMENT YOU CAN MAKE

Many people believe riches are as elusive as a slippery eel. However, wealth is a result, not a cause. Riches need to be attracted. Wealth does not come without your personal invitation. In other words, it is necessary for you to set proper goals and implement a plan of action in order to acquire massive wealth.

Actually, people have goals whether they realize it or not. The subconscious mind sets your goals, if you don't set them yourself. The following are examples of how the subconscious mind sets goals for people and programs what you do, how you feel, and what you become:

"I go to work fifty weeks a year."
"My job creates a lot of stress."
"I eat and smoke too much to relieve the pressures of life."
"I have no money left at the end of the month for investments."
"I work sixty hours a week and have nothing to show for it."
"I spend more money than I earn, just like my friends do."
"I'm doing the best I can, but I always fail to make financial progress."
"I don't have the time to accomplish anything."
"I don't have time to enjoy my spouse and children."
"I haven't got a chance to become a millionaire."
"I always made bad investments; other people have the Midas touch."
"I don't have time to read or improve my personal finances."

THE HIT-AND-MISS SYNDROME

Every thought that you conceive goes from your conscious mind and is stored in the subconscious mind. Listen to people talk, and you will observe them verbalizing their goals (intentionally or unintentionally set), which are implanted in the subconscious mind. People fulfill and carry out the dictates of the subconscious mind. What people become and pursue is a direct result of the goals set in the subconscious mind. Think how often a TV advertisement repeats itself before your subconscious mind, telling you to carry out the physical equivalent and buy the product or service? Repetition is the key to setting goals, advertising, education, learning, and building wealth. Never underestimate the power of setting goals in the subconscious mind.

As people think bigger, they become bigger. There is no limit to the capacity of a person's mind. You can appreciate the power of goals and the subconscious mind by analyzing the obstacles the last two presidents of the United States had to overcome to become elected to the most prestigious and powerful position in the world. People who become millionaires also overcome misfortune and defeat by learning how to control their thought processes.

The "hit-and-miss syndrome" is when a person goes through life letting his subconscious mind run wild and take in a conflicting set of goals and thoughts. The subconscious mind will ruin your life unless you program it to work on your behalf. Think of the subconscious mind as your "garden" of opportunity. The seed you plant in the soil of the subconscious mind will grow and manifest itself in the physical equivalent. If you cultivate the subconscious mind properly, you will receive and reap an outstanding harvest. If you leave things to chance ("hit-and-miss syndrome"), the bad seeds of negativism and disappointment will control your life.

HOW THE SUBCONSCIOUS MIND FUNCTIONS

The subconscious mind functions involuntarily, with or without your input and direction. It works twenty-four hours a day and carries out your thought impulses, similar to the conditioned responses of breathing, eating, sleeping, digestion, and so on. The subconscious mind receives your seeds of thought and automatically carries out their purpose. You must plant positive thoughts in your subconscious mind; otherwise it will feed upon the negative thoughts placed there through your neglect. The thoughts that control the subconscious mind will become a self-fulfilling prophecy. Plant corn seeds and you will grow corn automatically! A positive mental attitude is absolutely essential for your financial success.

Trade Secret Number 14
A person's acts are no wiser than one's thoughts.

CONFLICT OF EMOTIONS

Positive and negative emotions cannot occupy the subconscious mind at the same time. One or the other emotion will dominate your thoughts and carry out that action. Herein lies the beauty of life. You have absolute control over one thing in life—your thoughts!

You can only develop mind control through habit and self-discipline. The way you shape your thoughts, goals, and definite purpose will determine the financial position in life you occupy. All riches began with a state of mind. Whatever riches you create, they are first conceived in thought. All people are where they are and what they are in life by forming habits of thought that manifest themselves in like-kind deeds. Your thoughts will create and determine your financial destiny. The dominant thoughts in your subconscious mind are testimony to your present financial situation.

Trade Secret Number 15
Your thoughts give birth to the material equivalent.

Trade Secret Number 16
Not all past knowledge that your mind has accumulated through experience is accurate or true.

Trade Secret Number 17
There are no limits to the capacity of a person's mind.

HOW TO SET EFFECTIVE GOALS

The hardest thing in life for people to do is to set proper goals. However, herein lies the success of building wealth. Setting goals will give you perseverance, the ability to overcome temporary defeat, and the persistence you need to reach your definite purpose. Everything that you create starts with a thought.

The easiest way to overcome this obstacle is to embrace the thought that "you can do it right now!" Your goals should be written or typed and kept in a convenient place for you to read them at least every morning and before bedtime. You must visualize your goals, emotionally feel the results of attainment, and let them flow into your subconscious mind.

AFFIRMATIONS

You may write your goals in the form of affirmations.

1. "I am a millionaire."

Trade Secret Number 18
Visualize $1,000,000 in assets and let your senses feel and enjoy the rewards of accomplishment.

2. "I earn my fortune by investing wisely."

Trade Secret Number 19

Visualize yourself selecting profitable investments that benefit your personal situation.

3. "I have the patience and perseverance to accomplish my financial goals."

Trade Secret Number 20

Visualize "time" as an attitude of the mind that enriches everything that you will do and accomplish in your lifetime.

4. "I enjoy finding new ways to acquire wealth."

Trade Secret Number 21

Visualize yourself doing the following things:

A. Reading books and acquiring knowledge that unlock the special secrets you need to prosper.
B. Making new friends and having the "right" people help you.
C. Helping others and doing more than is expected.
D. Providing services to others that you are not paid for!
E. Finding untapped resources and intangible assets that build wealth.

The list of affirmations may include these and others that you deem beneficial for your definite purpose. Ten affirmations put into action should be more than enough to assure your success. The goal-setting process just described not only works, it gives birth to other benefits for a richer life.

Trade Secret Number 22

"Goals committed to action" is the process that will help thousands of people become new millionaires.

Establishing goals that place faith and belief in yourself literally works miracles in the subconscious mind. List your goals and affirmations before reading the next page.

Goals

1. ____
2. ____
3. ____
4. ____
5. ____
6. ____
7. ____
8. ____
9. ____
10. ____

In the event you want to be a "doubting Thomas" and decide not to commit your goals to writing and repeating them daily in the format suggested earlier, please do not expect any measurable change in your financial condition. The odds to become a millionaire will drop to "lottery odds" or a million to one at best.

THE POWER OF GOALS

Never underestimate the power of goals. The failures, the misfortunes, the road blocks along the journey to acquire a million dollars are converted into beneficial assets by the person who is "driven" by goals. You are what you think you are! Your goals will insure that you achieve that which you pursue. Once you start controlling your thoughts, you will be able to overcome the various obstacles that you will encounter on the road to financial riches. Your desires and thoughts committed to goals and affirmations will come to happen and become reality.

Trade Secret Number 23
People are worth what they think they are.

For things to change and get better, you have to change the way things are happening in your life. How do you do this? How can you keep your goals in focus to accomplish your mission?

1. Imagine that you are already in possession of your goals.
2. Believe and have faith that your visual goal image will definitely be fulfilled in due time.
3. Let your goal, in the subconscious mind, start working on you.
4. Your goals will ultimately drive you to success.

You look back at every failure and defeat along your journey as an activity necessary to give birth to immeasureable wealth and prosperity. Goals and a definiteness of purpose will change your life story from one of strong desires to one of reality and accomplishment. Once you firmly plant your thoughts and goals in the subconscious mind, the passage of time will bring your financial harvest. The seeds of your thought will grow and bear fruit in the same manner as the farmer who plants a good seed in fertile soil.

DEFINITENESS OF PURPOSE

The philosophy of financial success is as dependable and definite as the rules of compounded numbers discussed in chapter 1.

Establish a definite purpose. Write out your goals. Visualize your goals. Repeat your goals daily, and you will acquire the habit of thinking only in terms of success. The rewards for following this dynamic process will provide numerous ways to remove the barriers inhibiting your success.

Your definite purpose, committed to goals, will help to protect you against fear, greed, envy, indecisiveness, and procrastination. Your goals will become a magnetic force that will alert you to special opportunities. Your definite mission will attract and enlist the cooperation of other people.

Your goals and definite purpose will become so strong in the subconscious mind that you can succeed without significant amounts of working capital, without wealthy backers, and without a profound financial planning education.

Trade Secret Number 24

Definite goals will allow you to transcend self-imposed limitations.

REVERSE THE CONTROLS

Most people let their lives revolve around the world. They react to situations and accept their fate, believing that things could be much worse. Everything seems out of control and beyond one's influence. These people feel forced to smile and accept the fallout that comes their way.

People who revolve around the world live under constant stress and anxiety. This behavior manifests itself in the form of ulcers, heart attacks, and a worrisome life environment that fosters premature death. These people still have the choice and freedom of thought to say to the subconscious mind, "Stop the world; I want to get off. Time out! I'm going to regroup and control my thinking so the world will revolve around me."

Trade Secret Number 25

The world will revolve around you when you reverse the controls by taking control of your thoughts.

CONTROL YOUR ACTIONS

Let your mind and thoughts control your life. Make life yield the price you want. Avoid being easily influenced by the opinions of others or letting a television set, your neighbors, and the newspapers do your thinking. Let your ambitions to aim higher help you transcend mediocrity and confusion. Become a leader rather than a follower. Take control of your environment with your thoughts, definite purpose, and plan of action in lieu of becoming a victim of life circumstances. Life will pay off on your terms, if you take control of your thoughts and let your goals carry you to financial success.

Trade Secret Number 26
Most people without goals quit just before achieving success.

Trade Secret Number 27
Let everything you encounter develop into a learning experience for your benefit.

Trade Secret Number 28
Definitions of purpose eliminate fear, doubt, and failure.

Trade Secret Number 29
Temporary defeat means only that something in your plan needs to be changed.

CONTROL YOUR EMOTIONS

Earlier we stressed the need for you to have a definite purpose, set goals, and implement a plan of action to succeed. Let your mind control your thinking, and you will relate better to all situations in your environment as events develop and change. Your dominating thoughts and desires will always control your destiny.

Instead of getting ulcers because you desire a promotion

and your boss will not retire for several years, remember that stress and worry are first created by thoughts. Decide to provide quality service and do everything as best you can at work. Increase the quantity of services you provide and develop a spirit of cooperation with your work peers. Be a team player and keep a low profile. Contrary to what some people may be thinking, I am not asking you to turn the proverbial other cheek. Remember, you are what you think you are. If you want more, it is natural for you to give more of yourself in return. Amazing things will now begin to happen.

First, your mind is in control to make the investments that will accrue massive wealth. Second, people around you will respect your low profile and not view you as a threat. Other workers will be more cooperative and help share your work load. You will probably get promoted or receive a salary increase because "you reversed the controls," didn't complain, and were the only person who was not desperate and overly aggressive to grab the brass ring on the corporate merry-go-round. You should also be aware that most people who change jobs usually wind up with a lateral position that carries the same income and death-causing stress at the new place of employment. Become the big fish in the pond of life.

Trade Secret Number 30
When you take control of your thoughts, your financial fortune is independent of your salary and place of work.

Trade Secret Number 31
The human mind either builds or destroys.

THE END OF THE RAINBOW

Your wealth is determined by your investments, not just your place of work. Corporations and people lose billions of dollars annually due to employee turnover, excessive illness, absenteeism, and reduced productivity. If corporations instituted the financial planning concepts discussed in this book, employees would be happier, and productivity and profits would exceed all expectations. Why? Everyone would be in a win-win situation, and positive thoughts and actions would become the *modus operandi.*

Trade Secret Number 32

A positive mental attitude is the nucleus of all successful endeavors.

THE FUTURE OF GOALS

The goal-setting process encourages people to give more of themselves, to develop greater knowledge, to improve skills, and to reshape their destiny with a new, positive mental attitude. We live in a service-oriented society, where everyone is craving for better service. Give more of yourself than is expected or required, and your financial fortune will accrue more rapidly.

You will stand out from the crowd. The world will revolve around your definite purpose. You will influence and be observed by other people who will want to assist you. You will literally get back a tenfold return for being willing to put forth your best efforts, unsolicited! Get in the habit of doing things you are not paid for. You will be astonished with the wealth that will gravitate to you.

Trade Secret Number 33

Goals will pay you more than thirty-four dividends in the future.

Now, let's explore the financial planning process in chapter 3.

Chapter 3

THE FINANCIAL-PLANNING PROCESS

Financial planning is a dynamic, ongoing process that coordinates the activities necessary to help you achieve your goals and execute your definite purpose. The financial-planning process shows you where you are today, how you are, and helps you get where you want to go. Financial results are the measure of your investment success. The financial-planning process will also help you to reduce the risk factors, to save immense time, and to eliminate the stress that often shortens peoples' lives.

THE LAW OF INVESTMENT RESULTS

Generally, people do not naturally select the best investments for their personal situation. In terms of results, 95 out of 100 investments fail to do what they are supposed to do. People need expert help, and they are very concerned about ways to assure their future financial stability. Social security is not even an issue worthy of discussion. The reasons for comprehensive financial planning will soon become obvious.

We live in an era when most people will earn over $1,000,000 during their work career. For young newlyweds, that's a combined income of $25,000 a year. Yet, in this era of increased prosperity, only 2 percent of the United States' population is financially independent at age 65. Government statistics forecast longer life spans and increasing numbers of senior citizens, which compounds the financial independence problem. The need to save and build wealth is vital for survival during the golden retirement years. Hard-working wage-earners need expert outside help and assistance due to lack of time, limited investment knowledge, and their poor investment track record. All working people require and deserve the highest quality of financial planning expertise available.

Trade Secret Number 34

Most people listen to their well-intentioned, non-qualified friends, and make the wrong investment decisions.

Trade Secret Number 35

Enlist the services of a certified financial planner and other expert counsel to improve your financial situation.

With the help of a "seasoned" certified financial planner, and other qualified financial advisors with proven track records of performance, you can correct many of your previous mistakes and obtain the maximum profits on invested monies. Moreover, the expert financial advisors that you will select should all know and understand the importance of goals, the necessity of a clearly defined specific purpose, how to implement a plan of action, the art of repositioning your assets, and the proper portfolio diversification to meet your changing personal situation.

KEY STEPS IN THE PLANNING PROCESS

Your expert financial planner will help you do everything you would do yourself if you had the time, energy, background, and experience. The expert financial planner always places the interests of the client first. Your relationship and dealings with expert advisor(s) is based on trust and confidentiality. Periodic evaluation and review of your financial investment returns and changing personal situation are mandatory in order for you to build and maintain wealth.

Generally, there are four distinct phases of service offered by your expert financial planners:

1. Fact Findings—Goals and Financial Statements
2. Analysis of Present Situation
3. Development and Implementation of Plan
4. Ongoing Review and Revision

Phase 1: Fact Finding— Goals and Financial Statements

In the fact-finding phase, your expert financial counsel works closely with you to gather all pertinent financial and equally important personal data. The planner also helps you refine and crystallize your goals and definite purpose. You should be prepared to answer confidential questions on your assets, liabilities, net worth, taxes, future earning potential, goals (personal and financial), and investment constraints. You are your own person and free to answer or not to reply to any questions. However, the financial "doctor" can only make a diagnosis and prescribe the right medicine and treatment based on the information you provide. So, be thorough and complete to receive the right prescription.

It is helpful to prepare some simple personal financial statements. These should include a personal financial statement, also known as a balance sheet, which is a statement of your assets, liabilities, and net worth as of the date it is prepared. The following personal financial statement on chart 3 is provided for your benefit and should be filled in at this time, so you can determine what your present net worth is and what assets should be repositioned to better serve your present situation and definite purpose.

Chart 3

Personal Financial Statement of ______________________
Prepared as of ____________, 19______

Assets		Liabilities and Net Worth	
Cash[1] __________	$______	Mortgages on real estate[1]	$______
Stocks and Bonds[1]	______	Broker loans—Margin accts	______
Real Estate[1]	______	Bank loans and notes	______
Cash value of life insurance	______	Charge accounts	______
		Estimated tax liability[3]	______
Partnership or other business interest	______	Other liabilities (itemize)	
		______________________	______
Vested benefits in retirement plans	______	______________________	______
Other equity assets[2] (itemize)	______	______________________	______
IRA __________	______	______________________	______
__________	______	______________________	______
__________	______	Total liabilities	$______
__________	______	Net Worth[4]	______
__________	______		
Total assets	$______	Total – Liabilities + Net Worth	$______

Family Net Worth

Total Assets	$______________
Total Liabilities	–______________
Net Worth*	$______________

*Total Assets – Total Liabilities = Net Worth

1. Accumulate data in schedules.
2. Such as automobiles, jewelry, paintings, notes receivable.
3. Your best estimate of state and federal taxes due.
4. Total assets less total liabilities equals net worth.

In essence, the financial statement is a snapshot photo of your present financial condition. Many people are amazed at how much they are "worth" when everything is considered in the financial statement. You should make a file for your financial statements and chart your progress toward your specific $1,000,000 goal, at least, annually.

A personal income statement should be prepared to show

the allocation of income (salary and dividends), expenses, and fixed allocation expenses to arrive at the cash flow balance available for discretionary investments. You are encouraged to use the enclosed, simple family-income statement to determine how you spend your income and to find out what monies you retain for discretionary use at the end of a year. You can take the yearly amount and divide by twelve to figure out the monthly dollar amount available for discretionary investments. Your family income statement can be found on chart 4. Take the time to analyze what you earn and how you spend the income that you labor for twelve months a year.

Chart 4

Your Family Income Statement
(For the Most Recent Year)

Income		
Wages and salary	$	________
Dividends from stocks		________
Interest on savings, CDs		________
Capital gains	$	________
Other (pension, royalty, social security)		________
Total Annual Income	$	________
Expenses and Fixed Obligations		
Mortgage payment or rent	$	________
Automobile loan		________
Personal loans		________
Charge accounts		________
Real estate taxes		________
Transportation		________
Life insurance		________
Savings and investments		________
Contributions		________
Household maintenance		________
Medical		________
Insurance		________
Food		________
Utilities		________
Education Expenses		________
Entertainment		________
Total Annual Expenses	$	________

Total Annual Income − Total Annual Expenses =
Discretionary Annual Income ________________

Once you complete the family income statement, you may be surprised to see where your monies are going and for what purposes. You might even discover that some of your spending is "unaccounted" for on the income statement. Upon a careful review of the income statement you will be able to see areas where you can control your expenses and increase monies available for discretionary investments. If you so desire, you can complete your income statement on a monthly basis.

Phase 2: Analysis of Present Position

The second phase in the process is an analysis of your present situation in relation to your goals. Your expert financial advisor(s) will help you consider various alternative investments to achieve your stated financial goals based upon your assets, personal needs, and investment constraints. You might have income investments that need to be repositioned to equity growth investments that also reduce your tax burden. You will find that with a few changes in your investment portfolio, you have the distinct possibility of achieving your financial goals in a much shorter time span.

Phase 3: Development and Implementation of the Plan

The primary considerations in the development and implementation phase are to first accumulate wealth, then to learn the ways to conserve your fortune, and, finally, the distribution of your wealth. The 70–20–10 investment rule will provide proper portfolio diversification for you to acquire wealth, maintain the value of the estate, and realize the tax-favored ways to distribute the monies you accumulated. The development and implementation of a diversified investment portfolio is vital for your financial success.

Phase 4: Ongoing Review and Revision

The best laid plans of mice and men are not cast in concrete and steel. No plan, once implemented, should be viewed as absolutely complete and final. Circumstances change and the financial plan must be flexible and adjust to your new requirements. Not everything in your plan will work, but persistence in your goals, and changes in the investment mix of products, will insure success.

People experience, at unknown times, birth, marriage, divorce, death, job changes, shifting political and economic conditions, annual changes in the tax law, and new investment opportunities. These experiences make it necessary to reposition one's investment portfolio. Your personal financial plan should be reviewed at least annually and always provide the flexibility to adapt to changing personal and financial circumstances.

Trade Secret Number 36

The financial planning process will expedite and insure your wealth-building success.

YOUR FINANCIAL BLUEPRINT

Your financial plan is a blueprint that spells out in detail the financial means and methods for accomplishing your specific goals. This financial blueprint is highly personalized. The first step is to clearly define your goals and definite purpose. Your plan specifically documents, at a particular point in time, the exact strategies you have selected to implement. Your financial blueprint will coordinate an investment program that will counteract tax burdens and still provide for unexpected financial emergencies. Your strategic plan will decrease your tax liability and increase your investment profit yield by integrating your tax, investment, and estate plans into one manageable and highly effective program.

Trade Secret Number 37

Have the financial advisor coordinate the investment projections with your CPA or tax attorney.

THE FINANCIAL PROCESS IS AN ART

Financial planning, like all professional services, is as much an art as it is a science. It is a lifelong process nurtured on confidence and performance. The secret is to find the financial advisors who can help you the most. Hopefully, the financial concepts discussed in this book will assist you in finding the most beneficial financial advisors: certified financial planners, CPAs, tax and estate attorneys, and insurance and securities professionals.

Trade Secret Number 38

No one can become a millionaire without the cooperation of other people.

WEALTH BREEDS MORE WEALTH

Every year you are strongly recommended to fill out new personal financial statements. You will be able to see how and why your net worth is increasing. You will become more aware of your goals driving the subconscious mind to produce your financial objective. You will observe which investments make the highest profits, outpace inflation, and net you the most money after paying taxes. You will also learn from the mistakes you make. Because you visualize and repeat your goals, the misfortunes of life serve as pauses before your next financial success. Instinctively, you will develop skills to recognize and implement new investment opportunities.

Keep your financial balance sheets in a separate file, so you can monitor past progress and put to use new, emerging investment opportunities and skills.

THE PASSAGE OF TIME

You will have some outstanding years that exceed your greatest expectations. Every year will show progress because of your dedication to your goals and specific purpose. You will know if you have the right financial advisors, based on the annual review of the financial balance statement and personal progress toward the achievement of your written goals.

Trade Secret Number 39

Your success will become a magnetic force that attracts more wealth.

Chapter 4

THE TEN COMMANDMENTS OF WEALTH

The Ten Commandments of Wealth are common knowledge and practice for all millionaires. Working people who implement these time-proven concepts possess the necessary traits to become millionaires. The Ten Commandments of Wealth are:

1. Understand that everything you create begins in the form of a thought.
2. Establish your goals in writing and repeat them at least twice daily.
3. Define your purpose and start your plan of action.
4. Enlist the services of "expert" financial advisors.
5. Save 10 percent or more of what you earn and compound (reinvest) all profits until you reach your goal.
6. Start a self-directed IRA (Individual Retirement Account) and participate in other allowable qualified retirement plans.
7. Follow the 70–20–10 investment strategy to make your first million dollars.
8. Prepare personal financial balance sheets at least annually.
9. Continue to improve your knowledge and give more of yourself than is expected.
10. Share your "talents" with others who desire riches.

THE MIRROR OF OPPORTUNITY

The Ten Commandments of Wealth provide the attitude, skills, and knowledge necessary for you to gain and negotiate the competitive advantage to acquire and earn one million dollars. These commandments will work wonders provided you put these practices to use for the rest of your life. You can easily earn and become a millionaire before you finish your working career. What you give out comes back many times in like kind. You are encouraged to share your knowledge and success with other people who are also willing to give of themselves to receive a better financial solution.

Trade Secret Number 40

Incorporate the Ten Commandments of Wealth into your goals and definite purpose.

GET THE PICTURE

The Ten Commandments of Wealth do establish a practical image for you to become a millionaire. Your goals and definite purpose are like a camera lens in sharp focus on the financial picture you desire to create. Once the subconscious mind receives the impulse message, it will develop that film image into the physical equivalent of your financial goals.

For you to get the right exposure to become a millionaire, you must implement a financial plan that utilizes the best expert investment advice and help from others.

The investment vehicles and plans of action to help you become a millionaire should:

1. Reduce taxes and increase investment monies.
2. Yield profits of 15–30 percent or more.
3. Use other people's money.

ECONOMIC CYCLES

These investment strategies must work equally well in the economic cycles of inflation or recession, low- or high-interest rates, and increasing government deficits. These investments must also provide for working people to get started with limited capital.

THE PERFECT "PICTURE"

"Picture" yourself owning a million dollars or more in assets. "Picture" yourself making an annual investment of your choice that compounds tax-deferred 15–30 percent or more annually. "Picture" Uncle Sam giving you a cash U.S. government subsidy every year you make that investment. That "picture" is fully developed in its physical equivalent in the next chapter.

Chapter 5

THE SELF-DIRECTED IRA

Virtually everyone younger than 70½, who works for a living, can and should open a "self-directed" Individual Retirement Account (IRA). In the event you have a non-working spouse, you can even establish a separate "Spousal-IRA," which will be explained later.

The three major ways to get rich are:

1. Reduce taxes;
2. Powerful high-yield investment program (15–30+ percent);
3. Using "OPM"—other people's money to control capital assets.

The self-directed IRA helps you to achieve all of the three stated wealth-building objectives. First, let's discuss exactly what we mean by a self-directed IRA.

WHAT IS A SELF-DIRECTED IRA?

A self-directed IRA is one in which you, the plan owner, are in complete control of the investment decisions. You decide what to purchase with your plan funds, how much, and when. Your self-directed IRA should allow you to switch investments as often as you wish. Moreover, you are the only one responsible for the rate of return earned by the self-directed IRA. Your financial advisors can help you, but the control and final decision is always made by you.

ALL IRAs ARE NOT THE SAME

You can set up an IRA at a bank, a savings and loan, a mutual fund, a credit union, a brokerage house, or other financial institutions. But IRAs from different institutions are not the same. Some offer a choice of investments; most offer renamed Certificates of Deposit (CDs), with rates that can change long before you are ready to retire.

To get the most out of your retirement investments, you need to have the widest range of available investment choices. Select a self-directed IRA that offers a comprehensive list of acceptable investments such as:

- Publicly traded securities, including new issues registered with the Securities and Exchange Commission (SEC) for interstate sales;
- Money-market programs and short-term instruments including Treasury notes and bills;
- Real Estate Investment Trusts (REIT)—SEC, or state registered and publicly offered;
- Limited partnerships—SEC, or state registered;
- Mutual funds;
- Annuities issued by commercial insurance companies;
- Certificates of deposit issued by commercial banks or savings and loan institutions;
- Passbook savings.

INSURED IRA TRUST ACCOUNT

The self-directed IRA that you select should be an independent trust company, well established, and insured for losses up to 10 million dollars per incident. The IRA trust should also insure losses resulting from accepting stolen, counterfeited, forged, or altered securities.

IRA REQUIRED SERVICES

Services for your self-directed IRA should include: "on-line" computer maintenance of accounts; free posting of all contributions, dividends, and interest; easy-to-understand, quarterly ACCOUNT SUMMARIES reflecting all activity in the account; and no transaction fees. A one-time establishment fee of 25 dollars and an annual administration fee of .15 percent to 1 percent based on asset value is all you should pay.

IRA ACCOUNT COMPOUNDS TAX-DEFERRED

The monies in your self-directed IRA rapidly increase because the interest on your interest compounds tax-deferred until retirement. Over the years, you will make many different investments and receive dividends and capital gains that will also compound to build more wealth.

Tracking your various and different IRA investments and profits will be easy, since your entire IRA portfolio activity will appear on the quarterly statements.

As dividends come into your IRA account, you can self-direct them and any uninvested IRA cash to automatically be deposited in a money-market account or passbook-savings account. Thus, your profits will always be earning interest on interest and compounding until you have accumulated enough money and/or decided to make other investments.

The self-directed IRA gives you the flexibility to control your investment destiny and comfortably receive all dividends and capital gains in an orderly manner. The quarterly statements help you track your overall IRA performance and the investment returns for each and every investment vehicle that you select.

It does not make any sense to establish any other system or systems to monitor and track your IRA investments. The Internal Revenue Service (IRS) allows you to set up a different IRA account each year. However, one self-directed IRA account that receives all your IRA investments over the years and provides easy-to-understand, quarterly account summaries is all you need to best serve this purpose.

THE SAFEST AND BEST TAX SHELTER

The contributions in the IRA account are tax deductible from gross income each year, whether you itemize deductions or not. The contributions earn interest and dividends without current taxation, as long as they remain in the IRA account.

This combination of tax deductible investments and tax-deferred profits allows you to build a substantial amount of capital for your future financial security. Without current taxation, the IRA assets compound rapidly. Here's how a 2,000-dollar annual IRA investment will appreciate, based on a 12 percent and 15 percent annual yield for working people who retire at age 65. It pays to earn interest on interest.

Chart 5

This chart shows how fast your IRA assets can build wealth, assuming an annual contribution of $2,000.

Age	Total Contribution	Assumed 12-percent yield	Assumed 15-percent yield
20	$90,000	$3,042,435	$8,245,795
25	80,000	1,718,284	4,091,907
30	70,000	996,926	2,026,691
35	60,000	540,585	999,913
40	50,000	298,667	489,423
45	40,000	161,397	235,620
50	30,000	83,506	109,434
55	20,000	39,309	46,698
60	10,000	14,230	15,507

Trade Secret Number 41

Open a self-directed IRA.

Trade Secret Number 42

Encourage the youngsters to start their IRA the first year they earn income.

Later we will discuss specific IRA investments.

Chart 5 clearly shows the total growth versus the total investment (2,000 dollars per year) due to tax-deferred compounding of all your profits.

If you happen to be flat broke, you can still start your self-directed IRA by making weekly investments of 40 dollars, or monthly contributions of $166.67. Open your self-directed IRA immediately.

THE UNCLE SAM IRA GOVERNMENT SUBSIDY

The annual 2,000-dollar IRA contribution is also deductible from your gross income, which means you pay less taxes. The amount of money Uncle Sam pays you in reduced taxes is dependent only on your federal and state tax bracket in 1986.

Chart 6

The chart below shows different tax brackets, the amount of money you save on taxes, and the profit yield on your 2,000-dollar IRA, *exclusive* of the investment return.

Tax bracket	IRA Tax deduction	Tax savings	Profit Yield
15%	(2,000)	$ 300	15%
25%	(2,000)	500	25%
35%	(2,000)	700	35%
50%	(2,000)	1,000	50%

Read chart 6 figures again and again. The IRS and Uncle Sam, under authority of laws passed by Congress, are paying taxpayers yields of 15 percent to 50 percent or more, just to *encourage* working people to open an IRA.

This government subsidy allows you to get "OPM" (Other People's Money—in this case, your tax dollars back) to control additional capital assets.

The IRA growth at 12 percent and 15 percent compounds a good return. Now, invest your tax savings dollars also and you will become a millionaire even faster.

Trade Secret Number 43

Get in the habit of reinvesting all profits until you reach your financial goal.

MAXIMUM CONTRIBUTION TO IRA EACH YEAR

The maximum tax-deductible contribution is the *lesser* of 2,000 dollars or 100 percent of earned income. If you only earn 615 dollars, you can contribute the entire 615 dollars to your IRA. If you earn one million dollars a year, you can only contribute 2,000 dollars to your IRA. You may contribute as little as you want, but you may not exceed 2,000 dollars in any one year. If you do not earn income from wages or other compensation, you cannot contribute to an IRA.

MAY SPOUSES SHARE AN IRA?

No. Each member of a working couple may have a separate IRA. If each made the maximum 2,000-dollar contribution, and they filed a joint income-tax return, they would be entitled to a 4,000-dollar deduction on the two accounts.

Taxpayers with nonworking spouses may make contributions to two separate spousal IRAs. The maximum spousal contribution is the lesser of 2,250 dollars or 100 percent of the working spouse's income, split between the two accounts. Neither account may receive more than 2,000 dollars in any one year.

The 2,250-dollar IRA allowance may be split 50-50; that is, 1,125 dollars in each account. Any allocation is acceptable, providing that neither account receives more than 2,000 dollars. One account can have 2,000 dollars and the other 250 dollars if you maximize either IRA account.

DOES A SELF-DIRECTED IRA AFFECT OTHER RETIREMENT PLANS?

No. In 1986, anyone under age 70½ with earned income is eligible to establish an IRA, even if covered by an employer's retirement plan. This includes corporate pension and profit-sharing plans, Keogh Plans, 403(B) tax-sheltered annuity plans, and state and federal government retirement plans. Moreover, IRA contributions do not affect social-security benefits.

WHEN CAN YOU MAKE AN IRA CONTRIBUTION?

You have until your income-tax–filing deadline to contribute to the IRA and take the deduction for the previous tax year. For most taxpayers, this means that you have until April 15 of the following year to qualify for a deduction for the previous tax year.

DOES IT PAY TO MAKE AN EARLY IRA CONTRIBUTION?

Yes. If you can afford to make the entire 2,000-dollar contribution at one time, the earlier you make it, the better. January 1 is an ideal time and great way to start the New Year. The sooner you make the contribution, the more time to compound and accumulate tax-deferred wealth.

MUST PEOPLE CONTRIBUTE TO IRAs EVERY YEAR?

Yes and No. Congress has made IRA funding a voluntary deductible contribution, so it is not mandatory from a legal point of view. However, Uncle Sam is giving you a tax subsidiary rebate equal to your tax bracket as we already explained. You only get the tax rebate if you make the IRA contribution. Nowhere else can you invest and save taxes on all investments except for the IRA and other qualified retirement plans. So, the IRA is not mandatory by law, but the IRA is a mandatory way to reduce taxes and to build wealth. No matter what your investment philosophy may be, an IRA only helps you make more money and safely reduce taxes without audit problems.

IRA INVESTMENT RESTRICTIONS

The sky is not the limit. Diamonds and mink coats were allowed several years ago but not today. The IRS specifically prohibits investments of IRA assets in life insurance and "collectibles" including such items as art, precious metals and stones, antiques, jewelry, coins, et cetera. Earlier, we listed the money-making, approved investment suitable for the self-directed IRA.

WHEN CAN PEOPLE TAKE MONEY OUT OF THE IRA?

Unless you become disabled or die, the IRS assesses a percentage tax penalty on distributions taken from an IRA before one reaches the age of 59½. You are also taxed on the amounts withdrawn in any year, and you pay the statutory tax rate. However, you may borrow 2,000 dollars to make an IRA contribution.

WHEN MUST YOU TAKE MONEY OUT OF AN IRA?

You must begin taking at least minimum distributions from the IRA in the year you reach age 70½. The maximum distributions are determined each year based on your life expectancy tables and the life expectancy of your spouse, if applicable. Of course, you can always take more than the minimum, but if you decide to take less than the minimum required, unnecessary tax problems develop. The IRS can and does impose a 50-percent tax penalty on the difference between what you took and what you should have taken.

Remember, if you decide to take IRA distributions in installments after you retire, the account will continue to grow, even though you are not making contributions. This is because the total assets left in the IRA account will continue to earn interest and dividends, which also accumulate without taxation, as long as they remain in the IRA account.

Once you retire, you have the freedom to use the IRA funds for any purpose you so desire. At death, the IRA assets pass to the named beneficiary(s).

CAN CREDITORS CLAIM IRA ASSETS?

Generally, assets in an IRA plan may not be attached by creditors, nor can they be used as security or collateral for any kind of loan. Congress has made the IRA a "Sacred Cow."

CAN TRUSTEES FOR AN IRA BE CHANGED?

Yes. You can roll your existing IRA over into a self-directed IRA with another trustee. You can also ask your current trustee to transfer your assets to the new self-directed IRA.

The difference between a transfer and a rollover is that, in a transfer, you never actually take possession of the money in the account. One trustee sends the assets directly to the other trustee.

In a rollover, you receive a check from your trustee and then have sixty days in which to establish a new IRA and deposit all or part of the distribution you have received. If you decide to roll over only a portion of your IRA, you will be taxed at ordinary income rates on the amount not rolled over. Rollovers are allowed only once each year. The amount not rolled over will be treated as a premature distribution, subject to the percentage IRS tax penalty if you are younger than 59½.

You should transfer all your IRA accounts into one self-directed IRA for convenience and the ease of tracking your IRA portfolio progress on the quarterly account statement.

Your self-directed IRA, and other qualified pension accounts that you are eligible to participate in, can make you a millionaire over a period of time.

Trade Secret Number 44

Retirement plans allow you to accumulate a mountain of wealth on small molehill investments over a period of time.

The investment selection for the IRA should follow the 70–20–10 investment rule guidelines discussed in a later chapter.

First we will explain how to develop the "Midas Touch."

Chapter 6

THE MIDAS TOUCH

The "Midas Touch" is like a magnetic force that instinctively draws people to excellent investment vehicles. The Midas Touch has its roots in the subconscious mind. Anyone can acquire and profit from this Midas Touch by committing oneself to follow the Ten Commandments of Wealth. Take a break and reread the Ten Commandments of Wealth in chapter 4.

OPPORTUNITY DOES NOT COME UNINVITED

Opportunity is another facet of the Midas Touch. Opportunity is more readily available to people who set goals, have a definite purpose, and have a plan of action to build wealth. People attract what they are and what they believe they will also acquire. That is one reason why wealth breeds more wealth.

Trade Secret Number 45
All wealthy people learned how to develop the Midas Touch.

THE 10-PERCENT SOLUTION

The concept of the "perfect ten" is very big today. The first and most important step necessary to cultivate the Midas

Touch and to become a millionaire in the near future is to start saving at least 10 percent of what you earn. Save 10 percent or more of your salary. Anyone who saves 10 percent or more of monies earned, and allows the interest on the money to compound and grow bigger over a period of time, deserves to become wealthy and can become a millionaire.

Moreover, opportunities to make sound, profitable investments will now begin to come your way. The simple fact that you are saving the fruits of your labor draws investment opportunities into your awareness. Conversely, if you spend all of what you earn, opportunities for true, lasting wealth will rarely present themselves. Instead, you may find yourself falling deeper and deeper into debt and despair. The choice is yours and should be an easy decision to make.

All millionaires started out by first saving money and then reinvesting the profits earned. Your standard of living will not drop or change if you save 10 percent of your salary and live off the remaining 90 percent of your salary. However, your socioeconomic life-style will start to get better once the 10 percent of earning is invested and reinvested to create more and more wealth.

A common success story for over 90 percent of all millionaires reads something like this: "I had saved —— dollars and was able to then buy into or borrow —— dollars, which laid the foundation for the massive fortune I earned and now possess." Millionaires and multimillionaires still save money, and they have learned to keep their fortunes working for them. These people now need to spend only some of the interest earned on their principal to maintain their lifestyle. People who have money appreciate its value and strive to keep it intact, as opposed to spending and losing it. Once you start saving 10 percent or more of what you earn, you will develop the Midas Touch to reach your financial goal. People who display wisdom are rewarded by their actions.

CONSUMER VERSUS SAVER

Mass advertising on TV, radio, newspaper, magazines, billboards, et cetera, is constantly competing for more than 100 percent of what people earn. Nobody, not even a billionaire, can satisfy all desires. All people, however, can satisfy their basic needs of food, clothing, shelter, and relaxation (entertainment) with 90 percent of their salary.

Many people trick themselves by consuming and spending more than they earn. These people have a slim chance of becoming millionaires. The reason is self-evident. If all the wealth in the world was given to them, they would only lose it in a short period of time. Why? Most people who get something for nothing already know how to make something become nothing. The habit of spending more than one has will erode any mountain of wealth.

In chapter 2 we discussed "reversing the controls" to become financially independent. Saving 10 percent or more of what you earn is an excellent method to reverse your spending habits and to start building massive wealth. Some people routinely give 10 percent of what they earn to their church and still manage to save additional monies and become rich without compromising their standard of living.

Trade Secret Number 46
Save 10 percent or more of what you earn.

SAVINGS FORMULA

Realize that you labor twelve months a year for naught if you save zero money. Realize that what you sow you reap. Realize that it is impossible to harvest a million dollars without first planting money "seeds." Realize that all millionaires start by saving hard-earned money. Realize that you live in a consumer-oriented society. Realize that less than 1 percent of the population are millionaires. Realize that you have full control to determine your spending and saving. Here are the four steps to help you save 10 percent or more of what you earn.

1. Pay yourself 10 percent of gross earnings every paycheck.
   a. Set up payroll deduction to credit union.
   b. Set up payroll deduction to bank or money-market fund.
   c. Write out the check yourself.
2. Live on 70 percent of earnings.
   a. Food
   b. Clothing
   c. Shelter
   d. Transportation
   e. Entertainment
   f. Exotics
   g. Prepare income and expense statements monthly
3. Use remaining 20 percent to reduce consumption debts!
   a. Pay off one small debt each month.
   b. Consolidate all debts into one loan.
   c. Stop abusing and/or using credit cards.
   d. Redline impulsive "valueless" consumption.

Saving taxes also enhances wealth. Most people spend from 11–65 percent of their earnings just to pay federal and state income taxes. Depending on tax liability, people work from 1.3–6 months a year for Uncle Sam. This tax liability can be greatly reduced by taking advantage of the special investment incentives that Congress has legislated to help stimulate the growth and development of our economy. The IRA and other tax-favored investments that will be discussed can help you recapture tax dollars and increase savings.

Whenever you make an investment, you should and probably do demand value (profitable return) for your value (money). Follow the same value-for-value concept when you use your checkbook or credit cards.

Take a break for a few minutes and examine your checkbook and credit-card account sheets. Look at the things you spend your money on. Determine if you spent your money wisely and received value for value. The Midas Touch will become part of you as soon as you eliminate the worthless spending and replace it with meaningful choices of value. At the end of each month, place your checks into three separate files and label them:

1. Savings—10 percent or more;
2. Living expenses—70 percent;
3. Debt reduction—20 percent.

Do this monthly, and every subsequent month you will handle your earnings more wisely. Filling in a monthly income and expense statement will accomplish the same result.

The Midas Touch always seeks out people who set goals, have a definite purpose, and save 10 percent or more of what they earn. The Midas Touch is within your grasp. Follow the Ten Commandments of Wealth, and the Midas Touch will manifest itself in your investment decisions.

CHECKLIST

Complete and fill in a new financial balance sheet to monitor your goals, definite purpose, and investment results. If your net worth is not where you feel it should be, then review the Ten Commandments of Wealth to determine why you are off track. For instance, if it is a lack of goals, then reread the chapter on goals. Once you are back in focus, you are now ready to resume progress in the attainment of your financial goals.

The next chapter discusses the safest and quickest investment formula to build a million-dollar estate.

Chapter 7

THE 70–20–10 INVESTMENT RULE

We live in a global economy and in a world full of tremendous problems. There are complex uncertainties in our world and tremendous problems that may or may not be resolved, such as, huge deficits, bank loans in default, trade conflicts, and changing tax laws. There is also tremendous opportunity for those people who can see which trends of the past will continue in the future. One thing seems clear in practically every one of these major problems in the United States and in other nations. Specifically, these problems are not going to lead to deflation. Every problem is going to lead to more inflation.

INFLATION REVISITED

Since World War II, every year has been inflationary except 1945 and 1955. The cost of living in the United States has doubled in the last nine years. The United States government talks about the war on inflation and how to control inflation. No one ever talks about "eliminating inflation." In the years ahead, inflation will range from 2½ percent to 20 percent. Investments that plan on inflation will prosper in the future.

FORECAST FOR INFLATION

The 70–20–10 investment rule is based on the cost of living doubling again in the next nine years. This means real estate prices will double in nine years. Land costs, rents, labor, and building supplies will also double in cost. The 70–20–10 investment rule is also flexible to meet the following investor constraints:

1. Time and dollar commitment;
2. Liquidity needs;
3. Marketability requirements;
4. Tax-bracket savings;
5. Risk tolerance;
6. Portfolio diversification.

The 70–20–10 investment rule provides the structure for any working person, regardless of age or income, to develop a personalized investment portfolio that will appreciate in value to one million dollars over a period of time.

Trade Secret Number 47

Plan on inflation to help you make higher investment profits.

ASSUMPTIONS FOR FINANCIAL SUCCESS

1. The United States is the best place to live.
2. The nuclear-war stalemate will continue.
3. Private property rights will be respected by government.
4. We will retain large amounts of personal freedom.
5. The dollar will survive.
6. Free markets will exist.
7. Inflation will range from 2½ percent to 20 percent annually.
8. The cost of living will double every nine years.

9. People will implement the 70–20–10 investment rule to acquire their first million dollars.
10. Estate-planning concepts should not be based on government programs such as social security.

COMPONENTS OF THE 70–20–10 INVESTMENT RULE

The 70–20–10 investment rule is structured to provide diversification of choice within each category and to provide the safest and quickest investment strategy for working people to build massive wealth. Once a person becomes a millionaire, the product mix may vary, but the basic investment techniques will always remain the same. The component categories of this investment strategy are:

1. 70 percent category—real estate;
2. 20 percent category—mutual funds and management securities;
3. 10 percent category—entrepreneurial money for high risk/high return, active or passive investments.

Before we discuss the specific investments and diversification within each category, you must first implement the same philosophy of money common to all wealthy families in the United States. This philosophy was alluded to in the Midas Touch chapter. The philosophy of money necessary to build massive wealth has a logical sequence that working people can follow:

1. Earn money for services provided;
2. Keep expenses down;
3. Start saving 10 percent or more of earnings;
4. Develop a prudent, diversified investment program.

Each category, the 70 percent or 20 percent or 10 percent,

can individually or collectively make you a millionaire. Reread the last statement. You have several options to become a millionaire. It is extremely important, without the use of a crystal ball, for you to start investing in all three categories. We will go into greater depth and explain the diversification within each category and the reasons for each investment in the following chapters.

For instance, a person might start by buying a residence (house, townhouse, condominium) in category one—real estate. Category two might start with a 50-dollar to 200-dollar monthly contribution in a mutual fund with global stocks and bonds. Category three might be a 100-dollar deposit in a special money-market account for the purpose of starting a business, or saving for education and training that will improve your earnings. Category three might even be used to invest in new start-up technology.

AVOID THE CHOKE-COLLAR SYNDROME

The major reason that people fail to stay with a sound investment program is the lack of diversification and freedom of choice common to most financial plans that are cast in steel and concrete. Each category within the 70–20–10 investment rule is flexible and gives you freedom of choice. The 70–20–10 investment rule also gives you peace of mind because different investments have different cycles and timing periods to realize substantial profits.

The 10-percent category may bring you unimaginable riches or the excitement of doing your "own things" as part of portfolio diversification, whether or not it makes sense to anyone else. Many investors and creative people who pioneered new ideas and concepts that fit in the 10-percent category did so without public support. These people were discouraged by their peers, but they had the persistence to believe in their ideas, and many made huge fortunes. Others lost everything they owned. You may develop insight into a new product, idea, or marketing concept that will pay handsome rewards. We recommend that you pursue them as part of the 10-percent category. The 70-percent and 20-percent categories will assume the necessary diversification for you to succeed, regardless of the results of any one business venture.

Part II of this book will focus on the investments available to you in the 70-percent real estate category, the 20-percent mutual fund category, and the 10-percent eclectic entrepreneurial spirit category (for lack of a better name for the doing-your-own-thing theory.)

Trade Secret Number 48

Persistence investing using the 70–20–10 investment rule will bring phenomenal results in your financial future.

Part II

THE INVESTMENT VEHICLES THAT CREATE NEW MILLIONAIRES

Chapter 8

THE REAL ESTATE MARKET

The eighth wonder of the world is real estate ownership. Real estate investments are 70 percent of the 70–20–10 investment rule. That is because there are many diversified ways of gaining massive wealth through the ownership of real estate. Ninety percent of all millionaires made their fortunes in real estate. Real property is one type of capital that will always remain as a source of security and stability. Before we go into the select ways for you to prosper, both as an active and passive investor, you should know how the real estate market works.

THE "PERFECT" IMPERFECT MARKET

A "perfect" market is an auction market, like the New York Stock Exchange. Prices and market conditions affecting the supply and demand for homogeneous products are easy to find out. When motivated buyers and motivated sellers come together the market fluctuates and responds to the manifest laws of supply and demand. In the auction market, the market price controls what the buyer will pay and what the seller will receive. You either accept the market price or withhold your buy or sell position. You never get to meet the other party, nor does the auction process allow for negotiation of price, terms, and closing dates. No one can control what happens in the auction market. Therefore, one's desires and goals imperfectly fit into the market situation. Market pressures for equilibrium and the attainment of a correct price determines one's profit or loss.

Of course, knowing the right time to buy and the right time to sell is the ultimate rule in investing. Generally, one should do the opposite of what the "thundering herds" are doing. Usually the "thundering herd" is driving the new "peak" buyers to the slaughterhouse. Many people, without a clearly defined plan of action, invest for impulsive/greed reasons at the crest of a stock cycle and quickly lose their hard-earned money chasing Wall Street financial dreams.

Trade Secret Number 49

It always pays to search for underpriced property in markets that are also undervalued.

Trade Secret Number 50

The pursuit of long-term goals gives people the emotional staying power (wisdom) to overcome the short-term consequences of growth-oriented investments.

In the real estate market there is only one buyer and one seller for each property. Each property is inherently different. There is no such thing as one hundred shares of IBM that thousands of people can buy and sell. These market "imperfections" offer hazards or lucrative opportunities, depending on how smart you play and control the real estate investing game.

There is no anonymity in real estate. Both buyer and seller can negotiate face to face and shift prices "illogically"—higher or lower than market value. In the real estate market, I see price differentials occurring frequently, due to different circumstances of ownership, motivation, and knowledge. People have and will continue to make profits up to one million dollars or more from one transaction, just by having the knowledge and "expert" help to buy real estate below market value. Whereas, a distress, below-market-price opportunity never happens on the New York Stock Exchange. Arbitrage and market equilibrium make sure that the auction market price is always the correct one. Moreover, everyone shares the same common knowledge about the market price of stocks and commodities throughout the world's financial centers.

In real estate transactions, there is no central auction market to control prices, because no two real estate parcels and/or buyer and seller are the same. Each real estate purchase and sale takes place in a widely dispersed market, which makes market knowledge difficult to obtain. No duplex or single-family home can be "priced" like a share of IBM stock.

Location is another different and important factor common to real estate. Land is permanently attached to its place. New subdivision lots can sell out quickly, while a similar vacant lot in a less-desirable part of town can find no buyer. Location factors to analyze include: neighborhood, population base, visibility, access, the area's economy, and the political climate. Local public-information agencies will give you this data and answer your questions too, free of charge.

Real estate exists in a heterogeneous, regional market. National statistics serve no useful purpose and generally are misleading. Valuation and analysis of investment real estate requires special expertise to interpret many intangible variables. For better or for worse, there are no organized procedures and rules for acquisitions and sales. In essence, there are so many emotional, business, and economical influences on real estate value that these factors aptly make real estate the *perfect imperfect market.*

Real estate allows smart buyers to make profits by buying right and ever-larger profits by knowing when and how to structure the sale. The market values of real estate offer greater safety and opportunity for gain than exist in the more-perfect and liquid stock market.

There are several reasons why 70 percent of the aspiring millionaire's money should be in real estate:

1. Real estate investments benefit from inflation. Real estate is typically purchased on borrowed money; inflation adds

value to the property, plus it allows you to repay the mortgage with cheaper dollars. Inflation increases the rents on the property, and a dramatic increase in rental income also results in higher property values.

2. The zoning or the use of property can be changed, resulting in a windfall profit.
3. There are several ways that a passive investor can acquire property for long-term appreciation without devoting much time or effort. Real estate values naturally grow, as the community develops and becomes more populated.
4. Location can give properties a special value. For example, locations that provide nearness to transportation, beaches, natural landmarks, and convenient access to main arteries of traffic are all limited in supply. The buyer who finds these opportunities can expect greater property values, higher rents, and liquidity at the time of sale.
5. Real estate can be improved or "marketed" to gain greater profits, because it can be custom designed to fill the needs of the user. People will always pay a premium for value that fills an important need.
6. There are opportunities to buy real estate where the management by the present owner has been poor. Seasoned owners often neglect to keep rents up to market. Executors of real estate and trust officers maintain the status quo and often liquidate at ridiculously low prices. Shrewd investors who buy from these people can raise the rental income from the property and make tax-deductible improvements that greatly increase the property value.
7. Prices of many properties are often unnecessarily depressed by the sellers' demand for all cash, immediately.
8. Structuring and well-planned, maximum financing terms can result in a higher-than-market-value price at the time of sale.
9. People who own free and clear real estate or assumable financing can make special profits by selling to speculators who misuse leverage and want something for nothing, the so-called creative no-money-down method. No amount of

leverage can offset the stupidity of grossly overpaying for real estate with "alligator" carrying costs. An "alligator" is a property that eats cash instead of producing it.

Trade Secret Number 51

People who hold tax-dollar benefits too close to the eye seldom see the economic value necessary to build wealth.

10. There is no such thing as a good or bad real estate parcel. It is the changing, uncomfortable sets of circumstances that makes people want out of their real estate investment. People highly motivated to sell gladly make price and financing concessions, provided you "take" the property off their hands. These owners are called property "don't wanters" and panic sellers.

Unlike other investments, real estate can be custom designed and structured to meet your personal situation, investment budget, and other available resources. The Ten Commandments of Wealth work wonders with real estate investments. Control your thoughts and establish the goal and definite purpose to *only* buy real estate wholesale (below market value) or at market value if specific future changes in the property are imminent.

Real estate profits of 25–100 percent are available for the prudent investor with goals and a definite purpose. I know of several people on the road to becoming millionaires whose goal is to create 25,000–100,000 dollars equity per year by specifically buying real estate below market value. That goal can be achieved throughout the fifty states by being persistent and following the principles of this text. You can control what you want to do in the real estate market, and not just take what the market will give you.

Trade Secret Number 52

There's more money in real estate than there is in stocks and bonds.

THE REAL ESTATE CHALLENGE

Real estate is a field of great challenge both for the active and passive working person. In real estate, any individual with an entrepreneurial spirit can start with little capital and still make millions of dollars. Real estate will always remain a highly localized market and provide tremendous opportunities to build wealth for the knowledgeable investor working independently and with the help of professional real estate experts.

There are so many different real estate opportunities that it is often difficult for the working person to see the forest from the trees. Working people need to develop a strategy and a plan of action to profit from real estate. Earlier, we stressed that 70 percent of investment monies should be in real estate. The percentage formula that provides the best portfolio diversification for the working person is:

REAL ESTATE PORTFOLIO DIVERSIFICATION (100 PERCENT)

1. Individual (fee simple) ownership: 20–50 percent
2. Limited partnerships and joint ventures: 30–60 percent
3. Finite Real Estate Investment Trusts (FREIT): 20 percent

INDIVIDUAL (FEE SIMPLE) OWNERSHIP

I strongly recommend individual (fee simple) ownership for 20–50 percent of the working person's real estate portfolio for several reasons. First, every working person has a time constraint or lack of time to both work full-time at a career endeavor and still have the surplus time and energy to become a real estate tycoon. However, most working people do have the time to make a good purchase on a residence, a duplex, and a few small residential-income properties. The plan to buy one or two properties a year well below market value to build wealth and also to reduce taxes is readily attainable and does not have to conflict with your present life-style.

Limited partnerships and joint ventures provide excellent opportunities for investment in land, major office buildings, shopping centers, apartment complexes, industrial parks, agricultural, and developmental projects. These investment vehicles offer the working person limited liability (usually the amount invested), while the managing partner provides the "time" and "expertise" to make you a passive, profitable investment return. These investments are structured to give the working person immediate and ongoing tax benefits.

LIMITED PARTNERSHIPS AND JOINT VENTURES

Most passive real estate investments are packaged through a special legal entity known as a "limited partnership." This investment vehicle combines the best benefits of corporate and individual ownership.

The limited partnership has many of the advantages of a corporation, but it is not double taxed like a corporation. The cash flow, depreciation, and tax benefits "pass through" to the individual partners as specified by the partnership agreement. This unique arrangement allows the tax-shelter benefits of real estate to pass through to the limited partners, just as though those investors were individual property owners.

A limited partnership requires at least one general partner and one or more limited partners. The general partners are the active members of the business. They are the syndicators, builders, developers, and entrepreneurs who manage the business and thus have unlimited and exclusive liability for partnership debts for their share of the profits. The limited partners are passive investors and are not allowed to participate in the management and business operations of the partnership.

Although the limited partnership entity is treated as a partnership for tax purposes, the limited partners have a legal right, like a corporate shareholder, in that they have no liability for financial loss beyond their original investment. The limited partners receive cash-flow income from the properties, appreciation, and a "piece" of the most prestigious and high-demand real estate projects with a limited capital investment. The percent allocation for this category is a minimum of 30 percent or the difference between individual ownership and 80 percent of the real estate investment portfolio. For example, if only 20 percent of your monies go into individual ownership (20–50 percent) that would leave 60 percent for limited partnerships and joint ventures.

Category 3 is Finite Real Estate Investment Trusts (FREITs), for 20 percent of the real estate portfolio. FREITs provide liquidity, monthly or quarterly cash flow, and capital appreciation. They will be analyzed in a later chapter. It makes prudent investment sense to have 20 percent of the real estate monies liquid in FREITs, to deal with unknown future trends and changing personal situations.

SAFETY REAL ESTATE NET

Safety in real estate investment is manifested by buying properties (diversification) where principal value will not go down in current purchasing power. In well-selected locations, the property values will grow in value at least as much as the annual cost of living increases due to constant inflation. The right property location also insures a growing demand pull against a limited supply, which causes rental-income price increases and may also make the property more valuable by converting it to a different use. Moreover, property goes up in value based on compound interest and safely builds wealth due to its permanent place within the regional sociopolitical-economic system.

HIGHEST REWARDS

The most rewarding and profitable part of your real estate portfolio will be your individual ownership acquisitions (20–50 percent). Nevertheless, each category has its purpose in the master plan and will bring you outstanding profits without compromising your standards of safety, time, energy, and risk tolerance. The following individual-ownership chapter will show you how to eliminate personal liability in the purchase contract, how to negotiate and renegotiate below-market value acquisitions, how to borrow money, how to eliminate "alligators" (negative cash flow), how to minimize or avoid taxes when you sell, and much more. Take a deep breath and relax. You are in full control of your destiny. You can and will be able to control your thoughts, and acquire only what benefits you, to build and maintain your real estate fortune.

Trade Secret Number 53

Make real estate an integral part of your master plan to become a millionaire.

Chapter 9

INDIVIDUAL, FEE SIMPLE OWNERSHIP

Real estate is the "perfect" imperfect market because it is a local, individual people business. Individual, fee simple ownership is the ownership of every right, present and future, that there is in real estate, including the power to bestow any portion of this vast right on someone else for any period of time. Logic, common sense, and imagination allow working people to start from scratch and make real estate fortunes. There is a lot of opportunity for newcomers who know what to look for and how to avoid the pitfalls of real estate. Haste usually makes waste. Avoid following the "crowd" looking for fixer-up opportunities with low or no-money-down payments. These people are bidding up the retail prices and buying "alligators" (properties that throw off more expenses than income) that produce monthly out-of-pocket, hard-dollar, negative cash flow. Moreover, working people often do not have the time, energy, or cash reserves necessary to support a "personal" construction company to fix up an inherited problem. Money can be made fixing up properties by people who do it full-time and put their own "sweat equity" labor into the project. That's not a project that works well for the typical 40–60-hour-a-week wage-earner.

INVESTING VERSUS SPECULATION

Real estate investing versus real estate speculation is intended to be a long-term profitable investment. The investment property you select will possess these characteristics:

1. It will have an excellent location for long-term appreciation.
2. It will have leverage of available financing to reduce the cash down payment and will also have the rental income to support all property expenses.
3. It will be purchased at the wholesale (investor) price, to later be sold just below the future retail (consumer) price, leaving something on the table for the next buyer.
4. It can be immediately resold (liquidity) with proper marketing at a gain or to break even, in the event your situation changes overnight.
5. It has excellent "absentee ownership" management available if necessary or required due to a job transfer.

NEGOTIATING WITH A DEFINITE PURPOSE

People negotiate naturally for everything in life from salary raises to where one sits in a restaurant. Negotiation is an art in real estate, and the above real estate investing checklist forces you to buy in good locations, at wholesale prices, with prudent, leveraged financing, liquidity options, and net rental income economics to hold the property for a minimum of seven to ten years. The property you select should have the potential to double in value every nine years or sooner.

You have the choice and freedom to control your thoughts and to achieve your specific purpose. You will get exactly what you seek, because you are in control and other properties are available for the attainment of your specific purpose. No "missed" real estate deal can ruin your financial future.

The negotiation skills to buy real estate wholesale are easy to acquire. The three necessary ingredients to accomplish your purpose are: knowledge, power, and time.

Knowledge

You know and understand that you must be very selective to build a real estate fortune. You determine the location where you buy and establish the reasons for buying the single-family home or duplex. The price must be wholesale, because you are an investor subject to business risk. You also know that you want leverage of available financing, to reduce your down payment. The deal must be structured to avoid negative cash flow and "alligator" properties. The net rental income must support and carry the property expenses for several years. You have other properties to select from, and you will never accept a "marginal" property to build a real estate fortune. All good real estate buys will come to you in due time.

Power

You are a problem solver and the solution to the seller's problem. You are in a position to buy the property immediately from a highly motivated seller (don't wanter) who needs to liquidate or get rid of the real estate. You are even willing to close the transaction at a later date to accommodate the seller. Remember, that real estate is not an auction market, and your offer may be the only sale opportunity the seller receives. Always communicate the offer in writing, which forces a decision. Moreover, a written, signed contract is necessary by law to transfer property ownership. If the motivated seller accepts the offer, you made an immediate profit that will bring you greater financial rewards over the holding period. If the seller rejects your offer, the seller loses a buyer who can perform. You lose nothing, because you realize that you are offering too much if everything you present is accepted. Moreover, there are other available opportunities that you can find in local, regional, and national real estate markets to achieve your specific purpose. Have the guts and smarts to walk away to a better deal.

Time

Your time is relative to making the correct acquisition decision. Time is of the essence for the motivated seller who wants out of the property. Time is of the essence for you to spend it wisely, looking and bidding on only the best wholesale, real estate values. If it takes you one year to find one or two properties that you purchase for several thousand dollars below market value, you will become a millionaire in approximately ten years. Your time is rewarded for patience and persistence. The seller's time is rewarded by a quick sale to solve a problem. As a real estate negotiator, you are a "don't wanter" of everything that does not meet your clearly defined buying objectives. Always pass up marginal deals.

Your position is based on logic and sound reasoning. You listen and ask questions. You gather facts and ask more questions to determine what the seller who wants to sell really needs to get out of the transaction. People are people. You have already found incredible buys at antique stores; garage sales, when people are moving; and in hundreds of retail stores "going out of business."

Trade Secret Number 54
Your real estate goals are attainable.

RENEGOTIATION

You have the right to restructure an offer for an extraordinary buy. If you really want a specific property, perhaps because of what the planning commission will do to an area in the future, you can and should renegotiate with the seller.

Draft a new offer based on new knowledge gained about the seller's needs. In other words, there may be some trade-offs that allow you to maintain or, better, improve your situation. Never counteroffer or give the seller the opportunity to control your thought process. You have the time to find the property that meets your specific needs.

Once again, you don't have to follow the crowd and buy retail. I doubt that you would open a jewelry store business and buy diamonds, rubies, gold, and so on, at retail prices and count on inflation, future supply scarcity, and increasing demand to make a profit.

Trade Secret Number 55

Once you start acquiring value for value, your riches will grow faster.

Speaking of the buy-wholesale, sell-just-below-retail routine, several of my clients and readers now go to the diamond centers and buy precious stones wholesale (50 percent discount) and trade them just below retail for goods and services including real estate. All prudent business people negotiate to improve profits.

THE MASTER NEGOTIATOR

When you acquire a property in a good location with a nominal down payment, get your money back in a year or two from cash flow, and take cash out of the property periodically without being liable for the loan; you have arrived and deserve to be called an entrepreneur "master negotiator."

HOW TO FIND THE OPPORTUNITY

Now that you have written down your specific real estate investment goals, the next step is to implement a plan of action. Personal observation of everything in your marketplace is important, so you can learn property values. You should also work with third-party sources such as brokers, lenders, attorneys, accountants, post-office personnel, and consider using classified ads targeted to the marketplace you want.

Initial contact with experts who can help you is a small investment of time. Be specific about your objectives and establish credibility and good relationships with the right people to expedite your quest.

Selecting the right real estate brokers should be based on market expertise and the right "chemistry" to work in harmony with your objectives. You must always make the final decision on what to buy, to achieve your specific purpose and present the offer yourself. You should have "contingencies" in your purchase contract that give you the option to not perform in the event you find something wrong. Some common "weasel" clauses to get out of a contract are:

1. Subject to review and acceptance of operational records.
2. Subject to contractors' inspection of the property.
3. Subject to acquiring favorable financing within a reasonable time.
4. Subject to review by attorney or financial counsel.

Once you start looking, you will have several brokers and other professionals calling you about deals. When you look at a property that fits your buying parameters, you should gain the following specific information before structuring your offer:

1. Find out the reason(s) the owner is selling, how the owner priced the property, and determine what the owner needs to get for a quick sale. Every seller has a bottom line that will drop lower for a sure, fast sale.
2. Talk to the property manager and find out what needs to be repaired. Also, determine the human error in current rents versus market rents. Find out what the property manager likes and dislikes about the subject property, its location, and tenants.
3. Maintenance people will tell you what needs to be done and

the good and bad features of the subject property.
4. Tenants are a good source of information. Ask them why they like the property and rent there.
5. Have a general contractor give you an opinion as to the condition of the foundation, wiring, building, roof, and so on. You can have the seller pay for this report and credit you for estimated damages.

After you review several properties, you will visualize the ideal purchase, and the subconscious mind will drive you to accomplish that result. All experiences in the interim improve your knowledge and skills to reach your goal. It does not take much time to find one or two properties a year, as compared to the profits it returns manyfold.

WHEN TO BUY REAL ESTATE

The real estate long-term trend cycle is always rising, due to limited supply, increasing demand, inflation, costs of labor, materials, land, financing, attorney fees, and governmental regulations. Real estate does follow a business cycle, and there is a time to buy, a time to hold, and a time to sell.

The ideal time to buy is when the market is slow and everyone is trying to sell. The buy-low-and-sell-high cycle follows this principle even in the stock market. At the peak of a real estate cycle, prices are high, sellers are unreasonable, and the next phase usually results in flat or slightly depressed prices, until the demand-supply factors push prices higher again.

An important fact to keep in mind is that we are never buying the market. Instead, we are always buying a particular piece of property, which, for its own reasons, may be all out of cycle with the movements of other properties. The property's prospects are far more important than the status of the market.

It is the natural trait of real estate that it is a long-term investment. The future gains to be made depend upon long-term community growth and monetary inflation. Working people use real estate as a vehicle for long-term savings and capital appreciation.

Trade Secret Number 56

Owning a number of well-selected, long-term real estate investments is the surest way for the working person to become financially independent.

Real estate cycles of buy, hold, and sell come at different times in different regions of the United States. Historically, real estate has followed a cyclical pattern, with different geographical areas at different stages of the cycle at the same time. This allows prudent investors the advantage of seeking out property diversification in areas that are at a favorable point in the cycle.

THE TOP THIRTY JOB-GROWTH AREAS (1982–2000)

Invest where the future demand is obvious. Half of all the jobs to be created in the United States by the end of the century will be in just thirty Metropolitan Statistical Areas (MSAs), according to the National Planning Association, a Washington, D.C., economic-research organization. Among these thirty areas with the largest projected increases in jobs are some of the larger established metropolitan areas, including Atlanta, Boston, Dallas, Denver, and Minneapolis, and also relatively smaller areas with rapid growth, among them Austin, Tucson, and Raleigh-Durham.

Houston leads the growth list of metropolitan areas. It is projected to experience an increase of 1,268,700 jobs by the year 2000. Four other Texas metropolitan areas are among the top thirty: Dallas, with 639,000 new jobs projected; Austin, with 333,700; San Antonio, with 238,700; and the Fort Worth-Arlington area, with 218,300 additional jobs by 2000.

Seven California metropolitan areas are expected to have some of the largest employment increases by the year 2000: the Anaheim-Santa Ana area, with 1,004,300 new jobs; the Los Angeles-Long Beach area, with 841,300; and San Jose, with 643,900. The other metropolitan areas in California, included in the National Planning Association top-thirty list, are San Diego, with 533,900 new jobs; San Francisco, with 373,400; Oakland, with 297,200; and the Riverside-San Bernadino area, with 217,500.

Five Florida metropolitan areas are projected to experience particularly large employment increases over this period. The Tampa-St. Petersburg area, with 457,200 new jobs; and Fort Lauderdale, with 427,000, lead the Florida group. Other Florida MSAs, with large employment increases, are the Miami-Hialeah area, Orlando, and the West Palm Beach-Boca Raton area.

Although the majority of these locations, and of new jobs in the 1980s and 1990s, appear to be following the trend south and west of the past decade, several northern and mid-Atlantic metropolitan areas are also among the top-thirty growth centers. The Washington MSA is projected at an increase of 546,600 new jobs, and the Boston-Lawrence-Salem area is expected to gain 507,800 jobs. The Minneapolis-St. Paul area, the Nassau-Suffolk area, and Baltimore are among the top thirty growth centers.

National Planning Association bases its regional projections on an economic growth model of the United States, reflecting historical and ongoing trends and the projected state of the national economy. You know where the future growth will occur. Now is the time to position yourself in these markets for future real estate wealth. Time is on your side, provided you put your acquisition plan into action.

POPULATION GROWTH

More than half of the population growth in the United States will occur in the states of California, Florida, Texas,

Chart 7

MSAs with the Largest Employment Increases from 1982–2000:
The Top Thirty

Rank, MSA	1982–2000 Increase	2000 Employment	Percent Annual Change
1. Houston, TX	1,268,700	2,949,200	3.17
2. Anaheim-Santa Ana, CA	1,004,300	1,992,200	3.97
3. Los Angeles-Long Beach, CA	841,300	4,818,100	1.07
4. San Jose, CA	643,900	1,428,900	3.38
5. Dallas, TX	639,300	1,868,300	2.35
6. Denver, CO	630,300	1,508,300	3.05
7. Phoenix, AZ	588,100	1,327,500	3.30
8. Washington, DC-MD-VA	546,600	2,445,300	1.42
9. San Diego, CA	533,900	1,447,000	2.57
10. Boston-Lawrence-Salem, MA	507,800	2,498,700	1.27
11. Atlanta, GA	488,500	1,673,300	1.94
12. Tampa-St. Petersburg, FL	457,200	11,157,400	2.82
13. Fort Lauderdale-Hollywood, FL	427,000	845,900	3.98
14. Minneapolis-St. Paul, MN-MO	394,600	1,586,000	1.60
15. San Francisco, CA	373,400	1,378,800	1.77
16. Austin, TX	333,700	644,800	4.13
17. Miami-Hialeah, FL	332,800	1,163,300	1.89
18. Orlando, FL	319,100	698,800	3.45
19. Oakland, CA	297,200	1,093,200	1.78
20. Nassau-Suffolk, NY	269,600	1,324,300	1.27
21. Seattle, WA	266,700	1,127,600	1.51
22. West Palm Beach-Boca Raton, FL	237,300	515,600	3.48
23. San Antonio, TX	230,700	745,100	2.08
24. Baltimore, MD	220,500	1,309,900	1.03
25. Tucson, AZ	219,200	434,900	3.97
26. Fort Worth-Arlington, TX	218,300	708,400	2.07
27. Portland, OR	218,300	778,600	1.84
28. Riverside-San Bernardino, CA	217,500	768,900	1.77
29. Raleigh-Durham, NC	207,300	542,700	2.71
30. Oklahoma City, OK	206,600	710,100	1.93

Arizona, and North Carolina in the years to 2000. The states with the next largest increases include Georgia, Washington, Colorado, Virginia, and Tennessee. In the Northeast, Massachusetts is projected to have the largest population increase, and Michigan, in the Great Lakes area. Population is projected to decline in New York, West Virginia, and the District of Columbia.

YOUR FIRST REAL ESTATE PURCHASE

Without doubt, your first real estate purchase should be a residence (single-family home, townhouse, condominium, cooperative, duplex), whether or not you plan to live in it now. Find a good location and make that first purchase as soon as possible. Owning your residence has several wealth-building benefits.

FORCED SAVINGS PROGRAM

Earlier, we said saving at least 10 percent of wage earnings was essential for working people to become millionaires and financially independent. Let's assume you purchased a residence (market value $100,000) at the wholesale (investor) price of $85,000 with $5,000 cash down, subject to a $80,000 mortgage at 12-percent interest that is fully amortized and paid off in 15 years.

The 15-year, fully amortized mortgage on your residence allows you to own your "castle" free and clear after 180 months. In the event you already own a residence, you can increase the principal payments on the existing mortgage to accomplish the same result. Once again, do not follow the "crowd" and take out a 30-year loan that benefits the lender. The illustration above has a $80,000 mortgage at 12-percent interest, paid monthly for 15 years. Let's compare the benefits for you, the "buyer," with a 15-year loan versus a 30-year fully amortized loan.

Chart 8

Mortgage	Interest Rate	Monthly Payment	Years	Total Payments
$80,000	12%	814.74	30	$ 293,307.35
80,000	12%	950.63	15	−171,113.07
		Net savings for 15-year loan:		$ 122,194.28

The 15-year, fully amortized loan payment is $135.89 or 16.6 percent higher than the 30-year loan, but you save $122,194.28 in extra payments. The lender should also give you a "lower" interest for a 15-year mortgage, which increases your net savings. At the end of 15 years, with the fully amortized loan, you can live rent-free for the rest of your life and invest the monies that would have gone for mortgage payments. Moreover, you beat inflation and improved your lifestyle because rents will triple in 15 years and "your" rental cost is zero.

Your $100,000 residence purchased for $5,000 down, with only a 6-percent annual appreciation, will be worth $239,655.82 after 15 years. Remember, you did this with just $5,000 cash. All this is without considering the tax benefits of property ownership and using a conservative 6-percent appreciation factor.

You owe it to yourself to buy a residence for future forced savings, free rent, and tremendous return on initial investment. Remember, buying one or two properties each year with 15-year, fully amortized loans in itself can make you a millionaire in a few years.

A DUPLEX INVESTMENT

Again, for illustration purposes, let's assume you buy a two-family duplex with a market value of $160,000, for the investor price of $140,000, subject to a 15-year, fully amortized mortgage for $120,000 at 12-percent interest, with $20,000 cash down payment, strictly for investment purposes.

The land value is $21,000, and the building value is $119,000 for depreciation purposes. The IRS will allow you to write off (depreciation) $119,000 from your taxable income over the statutory depreciation period passed by Congress. Your down payment is $20,000, and the IRS will allow you to write off 100 percent of the building value of $119,000. Congress doesn't let your depreciate the land value. If you are in the 35-percent tax bracket ($119,000 × 35% = $41,650), your cumulative tax savings will be $41,650, more than twice the $20,000 down-payment cost. Uncle Sam is actually giving you back your down-payment money, plus a 100-percent return of the initial investment subject to a tax recapture when and if you sell.

The property value at 6 percent annual depreciation equals $383,449 after 15 years. Your $120,000 loan is paid off after 15 years, and the annual rental income cash flow should be around $38,000, 10 percent of gross property value.

You are also in the "banking" business now, because you have a free and clear $383,449 property that you can "borrow out," tax-free, $306,759, approximately 80 percent of the market value. Borrowing money or refinancing the property is not a taxable event. You can always "borrow out" monies, tax-free, against the property, as rents and property value increase. There are loan cost inefficiencies (fees and points) in this practice to be analyzed in your wealth-building strategy.

The cash flow from the duplex can be used to buy more real estate and also to pay off mortgages on other real estate you own. Remember to always reinvest the profits until you reach your financial goal.

Real estate has the special characteristic that allows one to change from one investment to another without a taxable realization by means of an IRS 1031 tax-free exchange. In a tax-free exchange there is no requirement that the properties even be in this country. Your residence can only be exchanged for another residence; otherwise, any real property held for investment (land, 30-year lease, duplex) can be exchanged tax-free.

Installment sale means you spread the sale proceeds over two or more tax years and proportionately pay the tax on the gain whenever you receive money from the buyer. Retired people favor this method, because they are not earning a salary, and they are in the lowest tax bracket. Please review this section to see exactly how small real estate deals, properly structured, can enhance your personal financial future.

DUPLEX BUYING SUGGESTION

In the event you purchase a brand-new duplex, have the builder get building approval for two separate legal units. Later, you will have the option to sell each unit independently as a residence and receive a higher retail price than you would get for a "duplex." Later, you will also have the option to "borrow out" and refinance each unit separately.

In the event you purchase a "used" duplex, you should buy at least 20 percent below market value to offset imminent repairs and the investment risk.

Recap of Duplex Investment

1. Down payment	$ 20,000	
2. Tax savings (35 percent tax bracket)	$ 41,650	
3. Market value after 15 years (6 percent appreciation)	$ 383,449	
4. Loans	-0-	
5. Annual cashflow (rental income after 15 years)	$ 38,000	and going up
6. Borrowing tax free potential	$ 306,759	
7. Duplex equity	$ 383,449	and going up

Past performance is no guarantee that the future will be better, the same, or worse. What matters is that well-located real estate always provides a multitude of profitable benefits. Our 6-percent appreciation factor is very modest by today's standards for well-located real estate.

It makes a lot of dollars and sense for working people to buy a home and put 20–50 percent of the real estate investment monies into individual, fee simple ownership. Residential investments are a forced savings program that dominates spending habits and pushes working people to productive ends.

Success is a product of faith, initiative, persistence, and foresight. The working person who has faith in private property, faith in our economic system, and faith in himself can become comfortably rich by investing in real estate. You don't have to earn a penny more to become a millionaire. Provided you implement the concepts discussed in this book, you can leverage your present situation into a million dollars by writing down your goals and starting a plan of action. Other people might not have the courage or insight to start now. These people will later give you their monies to invest, once your financial situation starts building wealth. You are in control of your thoughts. You are also your most important asset, with unlimited potential.

You can make it big on small real estate deals without much competition. Every real estate tycoon started with a "first" acquisition. Once you start owning properties, the odds shift strongly in your favor to become a millionaire. You now control a basic necessity that provides cash flow, equity build-up through mortgage reduction, supply-demand and inflation-indexed appreciation, and reduced tax liability, all for making a good real estate investment decision.

U.S. CENSUS BUREAU

According to the U.S. Census Bureau, approximately 9.8 million new households will seek rental housing between now and the year 2000. Locate the right real estate investment and negotiate for an "investor" price and favorable financing terms. Probe and find out the motivated sellers who don't want real estate ownership anymore.

BE RESOURCEFUL

Discover what the seller needs, and you can negotiate an excellent purchase. Because real estate is a local, imperfect market and a people business, many super opportunities are waiting for your offer. Be patient and you will prosper.

Some of the best real estate buys come from properties in the real estate multiple listing service (MLS) that have been overpriced and remained unsold for months. Remember, the little guy in real estate doesn't have much competition and can always find the good small deals. If you were competing to buy a prestigious high-rise office building, your competition would come from these cash buyers: foreign investors, pension funds, insurance companies, and syndicators.

Trade Secret Number 57

Today, as in the future, real estate will continue to be an excellent vehicle for great fortunes to be accumulated over time.

LEVERAGE AND BORROWING

Leverage is the use of other people's money (OPM) to control an asset. Real estate is usually purchased with borrowed money to increase the amount of the investment purchase with a smaller amount of cash outlay. Leverage allows you to control more real estate. Leverage should be used with discretion to increase your profits. For example, a $100,000 property purchase with $5,000 down provides $95,000 leveraged financing. A 5-percent ($5,000) increase in value doubles the investment value to $10,000 equity—that's a 100-percent return. An all-cash, unleveraged purchase for $100,000 would yield a 5-percent return due to a lack of leverage. Again, don't follow the no-money-down crowd, because the expenses and negative cash flow may make ownership a painful and losing proposition.

Leverage should be used only when:

1. The cash flow from the property can support the debt mortgage payments before taxes and after taxes in some special situations.
2. The borrowed loans should be fully amortized over 15 years to eliminate future debt and to dramatically increase cash-flow income.
3. Avoid leverage that breeds "alligators." Negative cash flow will not only eat your wage earnings, it will also destroy future profits.
4. You don't have down payment monies, and other people will put up the cash, to get you started or for a share of the profits.
5. You can find super buys and let other people put up the cash for half of the ownership.
6. You can leverage your time by hiring experts to bring you the good deals.
7. You can form an investment club and earn a noncash ownership interest for managing the assets.
8. You can enjoy the benefits of borrowing without being personally liable for the loan. There is no logical reason for you to be personally liable for real estate loans.
    - A. Property can be purchased where state laws forestall the collection of a deficiency judgment on a purchased money mortgage.
    - B. The property can be acquired "subject to" the existing mortgage, which makes the seller liable. Of course, the buyer must make the payments, but the mortgage does not become a credit liability.
    - C. The buyer can borrow money from lenders with an "exculpatory clause" in the mortgage that commits the lender to look only to the property for the collection of the loan.
    - D. In all states, you can use various kinds of deeds, the

terms of which exclude the obtaining of a deficiency judgment by the seller.

Why the extra protection if we are buying "wholesale"? First, real estate is a people business, and you and I can make a mistake. A totally unexplainable economic event, or an unfair political zoning change, could cause the property to radically drop in value. That might happen once in one hundred thousand times. Nevertheless, you want to be able to walk away from bad contingencies, without having the rest of your portfolio damaged.

One of the popular arguments for borrowing is that, with a given net worth, one can always buy more properties. It can make sense for a working person to borrow against the equity in a home to raise the capital necessary to make investments that build wealth and reduce taxes. However, any loan against the resident should be amortized and fully paid off within 15 years.

Yet, consider the fact that if your property is free and clear of debt, or even has a small mortgage, the lack of interest expense will enable you to accumulate money that much faster to buy your next property. And, in hard times, should you experience a temporary drop in income earnings you will not experience the fear and stress of losing the family "castle."

Another disadvantage of borrowing to the hilt is that it has the tendency to raise the price of real estate, called the "I'll give you terms if you pay my price" game. In cases where cash talks, it might be wise to buy first, then borrow against the property to pull your investment cash out.

Tax strategy reasons for over-borrowing and abusing leverage are opposed by the Internal Revenue Service (IRS) and many prudent bankers and lending institutions. Plans based on tax-shelter aspects will have uncertain results at best. Putting small down payments on highly leveraged properties creates "alligator" negative cash flow that condemns both the property and investor position, and requires a tax-shelter sucker to be the investor.

Remember, our purpose is to provide numerous ways for working people to acquire a million dollars. The get-rich-quick schemes may work in theory but, in reality, they usually evaporate into hot air and tragic nightmares.

OPTIONS

An option is a payment in cash or services rendered for the exclusive right to buy a property for a specified price, for a period of time that is forfeited to the seller if the purchase is not consummated during the option-time period.

Options can and should be used in lieu of debt as an instrument of leverage. Often, one can get an option to buy property for far less cash than the down payment required on a highly leveraged real estate purchase. The price paid for the option is all that one can lose for such investing, and, until the option is exercised, no ownership expenses start.

The strategy using options allows one to diversify and control more properties than available monies can buy. Often, the option agreement provides that the amount paid for the option can be applied to the purchase price when exercised.

The optionor can either sell the option to someone else for a profit or exercise the option and buy the property. An option is a capital asset that can be sold for long-term capital gain if the holding period is more than six months (in 1986). There are special advantages of investing in options:

1. Greater leverage with a limited downside risk;
2. The seller pays all costs of carrying the property during the option period;
3. The interest on a purchase money mortgage does not start to run until the option is exercised;
4. From the date of the option, all gains on the property belong to the optioner, because the option fixes the owner's selling price.

The seller pays no tax on the option money received until

the option is either abandoned (ordinary income gain) or exercised (capital gain treatment). Review this section on options; it can make you money. Having one or two real estate options on excellent properties is a worthwhile, practical, leveraged acquisition strategy.

For instance, you could option raw land in the immediate growth directions, which would give the land-owner immediate nontaxable option income earnings. You could later sell the option to a developer for a profit and also carve out a piece of the land free and clear for your real estate portfolio. You should also be thinking about options on single-family houses or duplexes when the owner needs some instant cash. For that privilege, the owner may give you an option to purchase that property, sometime in the future, at today's wholesale price.

Again, there are thousands of opportunities to make big money in real estate on small deals. Consult with the experts and start building your individual ownership portfolio slowly and profitably.

You know your present situation and hopefully you will seek expert financial assistance to accomplish your goals. You can make a lot of money on the small deals through individual ownership. Decide what percentage (20–50 percent) of your real estate portfolio should be in individual ownership. You might consider starting slowly, to gain experience and to balance your available time to find below-market real estate values.

Limited partnerships allow you to be a passive investor and diversify into real estate that takes big bucks to own. Limited partnerships limit your time and personal liability exposure to the amount of money invested. The next chapter explains why and where to place 30–60 percent of real estate portfolio monies in various limited partnerships.

Chapter 10

LIMITED PARTNERSHIPS AND JOINT VENTURES

Most "passive" real estate investments are packaged through a special legal entity known as a "limited partnership." This investment vehicle combines the best benefits of corporate and individual ownership.

The limited partnership has many of the advantages of a corporation, but it is not double taxed like a corporation. The cash flow, depreciation, and all other tax benefits "pass through" to the individual partners as specified in the partnership agreement. This unique arrangement allows the earnings and tax-shelter benefits to pass through (conduit) to the limited partners, just as though those investors were individual property owners.

The limited partnership entity requires at least one general partner and one or more limited partners. The general partners (syndicators, builders, developers, entrepreneurs) are the active managers of the business venture and thus have unlimited and exclusive liability for partnership debts. The limited partners are passive investors who are not permitted to participate in the management and business operations of the partnership.

Although the limited partnership entity is treated as a partnership for earnings and tax purposes, the limited partner has a legal right, like corporate shareholders, wherein they have no liability for financial loss beyond their original investment. This means the limited partners are not personally liable for mortgage payments and other expenses of the partnership.

Limited partnerships are a very popular investment strategy for working people, because they provide the benefits of individual ownership in land, major office buildings, shopping centers, industrial parks, hotels, apartment complexes, agricultural projects, and developmental sites, with a small cash outlay and without the time and ongoing financial operating responsibilities. The working person remains passive and controls ownership of property that requires extensive capital to acquire. The limited partner also "leverages" the expertise of experienced professionals to find and acquire the property, analyze the market cycles, manage and safeguard the investment during the holding period, handle the business paperwork, and, later, even market and sell the property for the investor's financial gain. The investment vehicle is ideal for working people who want to remain passive and receive cash flow, tax benefits, and inflation-indexed appreciation by owning a "piece" of prestigious and high-demand real estate.

Trade Secret Number 58

You don't need to be a Rockefeller to own, in part, real estate valued as high as 100 million dollars.

LIMITED PARTNERSHIP DIVERSIFICATION

Diversification among various limited partnerships is a sound financial planning practice. You should spread your total available funds over a number of different types of real estate projects. Selecting different locations and types of property will reduce the investment risk.

For planning purposes, you can design a limited partnership portfolio to meet your projected needs for tax shelter, cash savings, and appreciation. Understanding the benefits of each limited partnership and the track record of the general partner can make this passive investment a profitable 30–60 percent of the overall real estate portfolio. We must first discuss the differences between public and private limited partnerships and explain a little bit about how they are structured.

PUBLIC AND PRIVATE LIMITED PARTNERSHIPS

Real estate limited partnership interests are classified as securities, the same as stock in a corporation is a security. Therefore, limited partnership shares must either be registered or exempted before they can legally be offered for sale and sold through registered securities brokers.

Limited partnership offerings that have been exempted are referred to as private limited partnerships (private placements), due to the restrictions placed on the way they may be offered for sale. Public limited partnerships must be registered with the Securities and Exchange Commission (SEC) at the federal level and in the various states (blue-skied) in which they are sold. While the securities bureaus of the various states do not pass judgment on or endorse any investment, it is comforting to know that full disclosure is required in the registration statement.

The legal documents for a real estate limited partnership consist of three items:

1. The offering memorandum (private placement) or the prospectus (public offering);
2. The partnership agreement;
3. Subscription documents.

The purpose of the prospectus or offering memorandum is to provide the investor with all of the information required by law, including risks and conflicts of interest of the general partner, for the investor to make an informed evaluation of a particular investment opportunity. Unfortunately, these documents tend to be lengthy and full of "legal" boilerplate statements that have little meaning for most investors. The prospectus contains a general summary giving an overview of the total offering and includes the track record of the general partner, which, along with the general partner's financial strength and integrity, are the major reasons to make the investment.

Suitability standards for investors state the minimum income and/or net worth the investor must have to be qualified for this investment. Standards may also specify a minimum taxable income bracket for qualification. The subscription agreement usually requires one to complete a questionnaire, in which the investor acknowledges, in writing, that the suitability standards are met.

The partnership agreement is the legal document that governs all the relationships and activities of the partnership, including profit-sharing arrangements. Read the partnership agreement carefully, and make sure you understand the business purpose and objectives.

PROFESSIONAL ADVICE AND SUPPORT

I have not endeavored to explain everything about a prospectus, because I strongly recommend that you consult with financial advisors "qualified" in the particular investment area under consideration.

An expert attorney should be used in limited partnership investing to protect you on all legal considerations. The attorney will review the legal documentation of the partnership, to see if any potential liabilities or problems might occur due to the structure of the partnership or the paperwork. Good questions to ask the attorney are: "Is my legal liability definitely limited to the amount of my investment?" and "Do the projected tax losses and tax opinion appear reasonable?" However, never assume the attorney is qualified to assist you in areas beyond legal issues.

If your certified public accountant (CPA) prepares your tax returns, he or she becomes the logical one to review a tax-shelter investment, to see if it fits into your overall needs by preparing for you a cash-flow and taxable-income schedule. Accountants are deeply immersed in taxation and can render good counsel in this specific investment area.

Your selection of a securities representative should include an extremely successful and qualified financial planner who is interested in long-term client relationships. For that reason, the financial advisor would advise a prospective investor *not* to invest in a partnership, if the planner considered it unsuitable for the client. The right financial advisor not only knows the track record of the general partner and how investors in previous programs are doing, but his broker-dealer firm will do their own "due diligence" and save you time.

The broker-dealer securities firm, such as Carnegie Wealth Management, will physically inspect the properties, have their own attorneys and CPAs check out the legal and tax aspects, and consult with other outside, expert advisors to determine the economics of each limited partnership. The "due diligence" checklist of critical areas of evaluation includes:

1. Overall limited partnership format and disclosure;
2. General partner—syndicator track record;
3. Financial projection;
4. Financial assumptions;
5. The project itself (economics);
6. Risk factors;
7. Fees and general partner compensation;
8. Liabilities;
9. Conflicts of interest;
10. Suitability.

REPORTING

The general partner should provide the limited partners with a number of reports each year to keep all investors up-to-date on all matters of finance, operations, and property condition. Quarterly reports should include an unaudited operating statement that presents the financial aspects of the project. Shortly after the end of the year, the limited partners should receive an annual certified financial statement, and the K-1, which provides all the information to complete the partnership section of your 1040 personal income tax return.

THE PROFIT MOTIVE

Real estate limited partnerships are a people and product business designed to make money and provide other benefits for both the general and limited partners. The track record of the general partner determines the bottom-line profit.

Be more concerned with the investment return than the profit allocation between the general partner and limited partners. The general partner's profits are usually subordinated to a 100-percent return of the limited partners' invested capital.

The general partner's back end participation is thus predicated on profitable performance. The profit split may be 80 percent for limited partners and 20 percent for the general partner. Some splits are 90–10, 85–15, 75–25, or whatever the partnership agreement states. The split that will work best for you is the limited partnership that gives you the maximum return on invested monies.

Limited partnerships, both private and public, have provided excellent real estate investment returns for my clients. Since you don't have a prospectus or offering memorandum, and I don't know your suitability or personal situation, I will not name but illustrate a few, different limited partnerships, highlighting their benefits and track record.

LIMITED PARTNERSHIP 1

Primary Product: Commercial real estate—major office buildings in gateway cities across the continental United States.

Investment Strategy: Purchase attractively priced properties of outstanding potential, intensively managing them with on-site property management teams and creatively marketing the properties for an all-cash sale.

Tax Benefits: Sheltered cash flow paid quarterly plus 10–12 percent tax shelter annually on initial investment.

Holding Period: Three to seven years. Prior partnerships have held properties for as short as 13 months but no longer than 6½ years.

Track Record: Average annual cash return 41.9 percent—worst program 19.1 percent.

Minimum Investment: $3,000 per investor; $2,000 Individual Retirement Account (IRA) or Keogh Plans.

LIMITED PARTNERSHIP 2

Primary Product: National acquisition of residential income apartment and commercial shopping centers, industrial parks, and office buildings.

Investment Strategy: Income, appreciation, and tax shelter for three different classes of investors:

Class I: Investors receive 9 percent annual, fully tax-sheltered cash flow plus 10 percent of profits at sale.

Trade Secret Number 59

This vehicle is ideal for a person whose money is being clobbered by "bonds" and "inflation."

Class II: Investors receive 10 percent of the profits at sale. No current income but cash flow compounds at 14 percent per year.

Trade Secret Number 60

This vehicle works like a single premium deferred annuity or zero coupon bond with a 5-year maturity.

Class III: Investors receive no cash flow but get 90 percent of the profits at sale plus 100 percent tax shelter of investment over four years.

Trade Secret Number 61

This is an ideal vehicle to reduce taxes and build future capital gains.

Holding period: Approximately 5 years.

Track Record: Average annual cash on cash 30 percent—no percent.

Minimum Investment: $5,000 per investor; $2,000 Individual Retirement Account (IRA) or Keogh Plans.

LIMITED PARTNERSHIP 3

Primary Product: Raw land.

Investment Strategy: Purchase and rezone land, then develop commercial properties, office buildings, and industrial parks to sell upon completion.

Tax Benefits: Strictly long-term gains.

Holding Period: Approximately 5 years, first sale within 18 months.

Track Record: Average annual cash on cash 30 percent–no investor has ever made less than 20 percent.

Minimum Investment: $3,000 per investor; $2,000 Individual Retirement Account (IRA) or Keogh Plans.

Trade Secret Number 62

The greatest "immediate" profit potential in real estate lies in the areas of development and land assemblage.

LIMITED PARTNERSHIP 4

Primary Product: Agricultural land to grow kiwi, jojoba, pistachios, and figs.

Investment Strategy: Vertically integrated agribusiness to acquire land, install drip irrigation, plant permanent crops with a 50–100 year productive life span that are in short supply worldwide for annual inflation-indexed cash flow and long-term appreciation.

Tax Benefits: 100-percent tax shelter on investment plus partially sheltered cash flow once products are harvested and sold.

Holding Period: 5–20 years.

Track Record: Average annual cash return of 20 percent plus land values doubling every 5 years.

Trade Secret Number 63

It pays to diversify into land that also produces both a stream of long-term cash flow and appreciation.

LIMITED PARTNERSHIP 5

Primary Product: Residential income apartments in the microcosm of the midwestern United States.

Investment Strategy: Buy existing apartments below market value and replacement cost, increase present cash flow, and later sell for a good profit.

Tax Benefits: Sheltered cash flow plus 120-percent tax shelter on investment.

Holding Period: 5–6 years.

Track Record: Average annual return of 34.1 percent.

Minimum Investment: $24,000 can be spread over 3–5 years; $2,000 Individual Retirement Account (IRA) or Keogh Plans.

Trade Secret Number 64

All income-producing real estate should produce cash flow at the time of acquisition to maximize later appreciation in value.

Real estate limited partnerships are structured in more different ways than we discussed to meet the myriad of personal investment objectives. I listed just a few for food for thought; also, there is no guarantee that present and future results will be the same, worse, or better than past performance. Limited partnership shares are not readily transferable, so the investment should be made for the specified partnership holding period.

JOINT VENTURES

Two or more people often join together to accomplish an investment objective usually called a "joint venture." A financial joint venture is when one or more investors supply the equity (cash) capital and remain passive, while the other people involved supply the entreprenurial enterprise. Another type of agreement is a project joint venture, wherein both parties supply expertise as well as funds for the project.

Trade Secret Number 65

Joint ventures give working people who find real estate opportunities another way to make a deal with the help of other people's services or money.

Chapter 11

FREITs

A quiet revolution is taking place in the stock market for income-oriented real estate investments. That revolution is FREITs. They are proliferating. Last year, sales of this new investment vehicle tripled because of the benefits from an investment of one thousand dollars or more.

To be more specific, a FREIT is a finite life, self-liquidating real estate investment trust (FREIT). It is a financial vehicle, in corporate form, that allows investors to pool their capital for participation in real estate ownership. Unlike most limited partnerships, investors in FREITs purchase freely transferable shares of common stock. FREITs were authorized by Congress to give the small investor the opportunity to realize the financial benefits of real estate investments previously available only to institutions and wealthier individuals. A minimum investment can be as little as a thousand dollars, making it affordable for most investors.

Through an "equity" FREIT, people can participate in large, income-producing, commercial real estate investments that are managed by knowledgeable, experienced professionals. Not all FREITs are created equal! In order to maximize the opportunity for a substantial "real rate of return" on investment, an "equity" FREIT that features the following benefits should be considered:

FREIT Investment Benefits

1. *Liquidity:* Investors in publicly held FREITs purchase shares of stock. These shares are freely transferable and may be traded on the American Stock Exchange after the initial offering. Therefore, this type of real estate investment is fully liquid. Market liquidity is a feature *not* found in direct ownership of real estate or in most real estate limited partnerships.
2. *Self-liquidating, finite life:* FREITs are self-liquidating and have a finite life of 5–10 years. When a property is sold or refinanced, that cash cannot be reinvested and must be distributed to the shareholder/investors. As properties are sold and cash distributed, a FREIT self-liquidates.
3. *Cash dividends:* Investors in a FREIT should immediately start receiving a regular cash dividend. This dividend should be at least 7 percent per annum, paid quarterly and increasing as the rental income of the FREIT increases.
4. *Dividends are tax sheltered:* Investors in equity FREITs are able to receive a portion of their cash dividends tax-free, due to depreciation deductions on the real estate holdings.
5. *Investment growth:* In a well-managed equity FREIT, there is an outstanding opportunity for capital appreciation. When properties in the investment portfolio are sold for more than their purchase cost, the profit must be distributed to the FREITs shareholders. This "equity" FREIT will acquire a diversified portfolio of existing, income-producing, commercial real estate in varied geographic-demographic growth regions throughout the U.S.
6. *Annual appraisals:* Each year, all of the properties acquired by the equity FREIT should be independently appraised. These appraisals will provide shareholders with an excellent basis for evaluating their investment.
7. *Professional management:* To be successful, equity FREITs should have professional management with extensive experience in all phases of the real estate cycle including buying, developing, managing, leasing, and selling prop-

erties. In addition, FREITs must have an independent Board of Trustees representing the investors and providing checks and balances on management.

8. *Ideal for taxpayers:* With only a one thousand dollar minimum initial investment requirement, partially tax-sheltered income, and the opportunity for substantial long-term capital appreciation, an equity FREIT is an excellent choice for a low-risk, conservative investment.
9. *Appropriate for tax-exempt investors:* FREIT benefits can include:
   - No Unrelated Business Taxable Income (UBTI);
   - Publicly traded shares and annual appraisals to provide timely, accurate valuations; and
   - FREITs are suitable for investment under ERISA diversification requirements.
10. *Ideal for IRA investment:* Most FREITs offer IRA and pension and profit-sharing prototypes plans at reduced fees.

FREIT shareholders receive stock certificates and regular dividend checks that may be reinvested, tax information, and timely trust reports and communications. A good FREIT should always keep its shareholders informed on the progress of their investment.

FREITs should be at least 20 percent of the real estate portfolio, for liquidity reasons and prudent diversification for people of all ages who need inflation protection, tax-indexed cash flow, and capital appreciation.

The 10-year average annual return for recommended FREITs has been 30 percent, with no FREIT returning less than a 20-percent annual return.

Trade Secret Number 66

FREITs are a growth and income investment vehicle suitable for people of all ages and pension funds.

Chapter 12

MUTUAL FUNDS: THE WAY TO BEAT WALL STREET

Mutual funds have achieved tremendous working-people and pension-fund acceptance, by being responsive to specific investor objectives. In the quest for financial security, savers and investors need to accumulate wealth for retirement, college education, a business purpose, and other important considerations.

Virtually every investment objective, technique, and alternative can be satisfied by different mutual funds, from investing for capital appreciation to investing for income, from leveraging the purchase of a security to writing options, from guaranteed U.S. Government Securities such as Ginnie Mae's and Treasury Bills to tax-free municipal bond funds, and much more.

Wage-earners can choose mutual fund products that closely match their own risk/reward perceptions. The working person can start investing with a little money and gain the advantage of portfolio diversification, professional management, liquidity, reinvestment of dividends and gains, exchange privileges in groups, dollar-cost averaging, and convenient, peace-of-mind, passive investing.

Working people need and deserve a good investment return without the endless time-intensive hassle of understanding and competing with the large institutional investors of Wall Street. In fact, many Wall Street experts are dumbfounded as to why small investors, including stockbrokers, try to play big-stakes poker with a few chips when the track record and superior performance of mutual funds is public knowledge.

DOLLAR-COST AVERAGING

Dollar-cost averaging allows the working person to invest equal amounts of money (direct from payroll or checking account) in mutual fund shares at regular intervals. Thus, the wage-earner's money buys more shares when prices are down and fewer shares when prices are higher. Thus, the average cost per share is always below the average price at which shares are purchased. If the market continually drops, and never recovers, no one will make money.

Dollar-cost averaging (DCA) is a proven method of making the ups and downs of the market work for you. With DCA you can turn declines into opportunities. DCA is simply a long-term program, 5–10 years or more, of investing a fixed sum at regular intervals regardless of market conditions—for example, $100 every month, or $500 every quarter, or $2,000 once a year for an IRA.

Monthly investments usually produce the highest end results; quarterly, the second highest; and annually, third highest. DCA isn't a gimmick. It works because it always buys more of the cheaper shares and less of the expensive shares. That means your average cost per share is lower than the average selling price.

Chart 9

DCA Example

Total Dollars Invested	Average Price per Share	Total Shares Bought	Average Cost per Share
$100	$30.00	3.333	You invested $600
$100	$25.00	4.000	
$100	$20.00	5.000	
$100	$15.00	6.667	
$100	$10.00	10.000	You bought 49 shares
$100	$ 5.00	20.000	
$600	$17.50	49.000	$12.24

Your average *cost* per sharae was $12.24.
Your average *price* per share was $17.50.

Be persistent and your dollar-cost averaging program should work well over the long term. Consistency is the key to success. Look at market declines as opportunities to acquire more shares at lower prices.

PROFESSIONAL MANAGEMENT

The full-time professional management of investments in a mutual fund provides careful selection, diversification, and continuous supervision of securities backed by specialized skills, resources of information and facilities, and the "time" to make qualified investment decisions. The intense and constant search for the best of relative values is absolutely necessary due to the broadness and diversity of the marketplace.

For this professional management, in load and no-load

funds, the individual shareholders pay a fee usually measured by a percentage of the total fund assets under management. The details of professional management, advisory fees, investment objectives, and track record of all mutual funds are found in the prospectus and periodic reports to shareholders. The basic element underlying all professional management, in the supervision of investments, is the continuing correlation between the portfolio composition and the stated "long-term" objectives of the mutual fund and its shareholders.

In the investment research process, experienced analysts conduct a constant appraisal of portfolio securities in terms of three distinct factors:

1. General economic conditions;
2. The outlook for various industries;
3. The prospects of individual companies, which are analyzed in terms of management, policies, sales and earnings records, competitive position, and other factors.

PUBLIC AWARENESS

Several sources of information on mutual funds are readily available. From these sources you can easily determine a fund's investment objectives and philosophy, study the current portfolio composition, and see how the mutual fund has historically performed compared to other mutual funds with similar investment objectives. This process enables the working person to intelligently and conveniently select the proper mutual or funds that meet personal investment needs without spending or wasting a lot of valuable time.

THE FABLE OF THE ROADRUNNER, THE HEDGEHOG, AND THE FOX

The Roadrunner

The "roadrunner" has a system to make a "killing" in the stock market based on a "can't-miss investment strategy" secretly learned by attending several Wall Street cocktail parties and meeting a stockbroker who had special "insider" information. The roadrunner didn't have any specific investment objectives except to be a Wall Street trader in "hot issues." This swift-running bird's seeds of wisdom told him to "churn," to minimize losses and to pyramid profits. The roadrunner knew it was just a matter of time until a vast fortune would be made in the stock market.

The Hedgehog

The "hedgehog" knew inflation was destroying savings in the bank, so he became an avid reader of the mutual fund rating services to "ferret" out the best performing mutual fund. The hedgehog developed a sense of security by following and joining the winning shareholders. On January 1 each year, the hedgehog's New Year's resolution was to start the year by "churning" his entire mutual fund portfolio assets into the number one performing fund for the previous year. The hedgehog religiously followed the philosophy of only doing business with the best mutual funds for a decade. All dividends and gains were reinvested to compound investment profits.

The Fox

The "fox" had definite investment purpose, read the prospectus, and learned that mutual funds are an excellent long-term investment that one could borrow against in the event of a cash emergency, without liquidating the fund. The fox selected a growth fund with a consistent track record. The fox was busy making money on other deals, so part of his salary went into a monthly dollar-cost averaging plan that automatically reinvested all dividends and gains.

Judgment Day

Here's what happened ten years later. The "roadrunner" lost all his investment chips and got a divorce when his wife had to pawn a diamond ring and other fine things of life to cover a margin call on gold and silver futures. Five years later, the roadrunner began to buy mutual funds, which have substantially increased in value, thanks to his new "mentor" wife. The stockbroker, upon learning where his wealthy clients made big money investing, quit Wall Street and now functions as a real estate broker who invests 100 percent of all available capital in real estate.

The "hedgehog" doesn't have to burrow for food because the profits from ten years of annually switching to the top mutual funds significantly outpaced inflation and the stock market performance.

The "fox" now owns half of Manhattan, because he followed the 70–20–10 investment rule with two important modifications:

1. He personally syndicated, as general partner, all the limited partnerships in real estate.
2. The 10-percent entrepreneurial part of portfolio diversification also made superbucks, because the fox syndicated highly profitable new robotics and telecommunication technology.

The fox didn't leave any profits on the table with the mutual fund investments either. By having the patience and persistence to leave his one mutual fund alone during mutual fund cycles, the fox earned 50 percent more profits than the hedgehog.

It is never too late to profit from the experiences of roadrunners, hedgehogs, and the entrepreneurial fox.

RECAP

Dollar-cost averaging is an intelligent, convenient, and conservative growth-investment mutual-fund vehicle for 20 percent of your investment chips. There may be some reason to select an "independent portfolio manager," but that usually requires a large investment to secure, "possibly," the same results. The stock market does outpace inflation, but the safest, better-performing investment choice is the mutual fund designed to meet your needs.

We live in a global economy and monetary system. Part of your mutual fund monies should logically be in a worldwide portfolio that seeks investment opportunities in all types of securities issued by companies or governments of any nation. Many of the overseas markets have outperformed the United States over both the long and the short term.

Trade Secret Number 67

Your plain vanilla mutual fund will still be earning maximum profits when the latest glamour stock takes a dive.

Chapter 13

ESTATE PLANNING WITH A LIVING TRUST

Informed working people and practically all the millionaires use trusts, for estate planning purposes, that are custom designed by expert trust attorneys. Oliver Wendell Holmes once said, "Don't put your trust in money; put your money in trust."

A "trust" is a fiduciary arrangement set up by someone—call the grantor, creator, or settlor of the trust—whereby a person, corporation, or other organization—called the trustee—has legal title to property placed in the trust by the grantor. The trustee holds and manages the property—technically called the trust corpus or principal—for the benefit of someone else—called the beneficiary of the trust—who has equitable title to trust property. Thus, the essence of the trust relationship is the placing of legal title to property with a trustee who is to administer the property, as a fiduciary, for the benefit of the trust beneficiary(s).

There are various kinds of trusts; for personal financial planning concerns, the most important ones are:

1. A "living or inter vivos revocable trust," which is a personal trust that individuals and families create during their lifetime to benefit themselves or someone else.
2. A "testamentary trust" is a personal trust created under a person's will that, like the will, does not become effective until after the creator's death.

3. An "insurance trust" is a particular kind of living trust whose corpus or principal consists partly or wholly of life insurance policies during the insured's lifetime and/or life insurance proceeds after the insured's death.

Trusts can be revocable or irrevocable, depending on the purpose. A "revocable trust" is one in which the creator reserves the right to revoke or amend the trust. In other words, the creator has the flexibility to change the revocable trust or terminate it and get the property back. For the purpose of the aspiring millionaires and working people, we will only discuss the strategy and reasons for creating a "revocable living trust."

Preparing a sound plan for your family's financial future is not a task for an amateur or do-it-yourself person, despite widely circulated claims on how to avoid probate. All families, including yours, face the threat of substantial financial loss due to the expenses involved in estate settlement when people die. These expenses are loosely termed costs of "probate," although probate really refers only to the process of establishing the validity of a will in court. Nevertheless, the importance of reducing settlement costs and avoiding probate has long been clear to astute individuals and their lawyers. Revocable living trusts have for many years been a recommended way to minimize the delays, difficulties, and costs that so often complicate the settlement of an estate. A well-drawn revocable living trust structured by an expert lawyer offers so many advantages that the avoidance of probate is just one positive benefit.

There are a number of good, possible reasons for creating trusts; some of the most popular are:

1. To place the burdens of property and investment management in the hands of an experienced trustee, rather than leaving them to the creator, his or her family, or heirs.
2. To allow the trustee to use his, her, or its discretion (as a fiduciary) in handling trust property for the benefit of the creator, his or her family, or dependents.
3. To protect the creator's family or dependents against demands and entreaties made by well-meaning or, perhaps,

not-so-well-meaning family members, friends, spouses, spouses-to-be, and the like.

4. To provide a way of giving or leaving property to minors so that the trustee can manage it for them until they are old enough to handle the property themselves. This avoids the legal rigidities and practical problems of having to have a legal guardian appointed for a minor by the court.
5. To protect trust beneficiaries against themselves when they are physically, mentally, or emotionally unable to manage property themselves. Trusts are created to guard against incompetence and to protect spendthrifts from themselves.
6. To provide professional investment and property management for the creator himself (or herself) during his (or her) lifetime. This can provide proper investment diversification and the evaluation of the co-trustee's performance.
7. To manage a business interest after the owner's death until it can be sold or until one of his or her heirs can take over.
8. To provide an extremely useful device for setting up tax-savings plans, which is a big reason for creating many trusts today.
9. To provide continuity in management, assure privacy, and prevent will challenges.
10. To reduce estate settlement expenses and delays.
11. To eliminate financial routine and to coordinate all assets in an efficient, unified plan.
12. To know that your final decisions live on after death without interrupting the estate you built. You have the right to have your wishes executed after your death.

CORNERSTONE OF FINANCIAL SECURITY

The living trust that you rely on now can be continued after your death for the benefit of your family. Continuation of the trust would provide your family with:

1. experienced management;
2. payment of benefits with no interruption;
3. none of the delays and costs of probate; and
4. privacy at a time when it is needed.

Finally, your trust can be used to coordinate other assets. Life insurance proceeds or retirement benefits can be paid into the trust. Assets can be "poured over" from your will to the trust. Your trust can be the cornerstone upon which your family's security can be built.

MINIMIZING ESTATE TAXES

The revocable living trust not only saves on costs, but it can be drawn with provisions that minimize federal estate taxes. Assets in a revocable living trust, like other assets, normally are subject to federal estate tax upon the death of the creator of the trust. However, the trust assets need not be taxed a second time when, upon the death of the lifetime beneficiary, the trust terminates and the principal is distributed to a third person. The key to tax savings is that the assets in the trust are never "owned" by the lifetime beneficiary and never become part of the beneficiary's estate.

Thanks to favorable provisions of the federal estate tax law, the estates of a vast majority of people will not have to pay any estate tax. If you do have an estate tax liability, trust funds can pass to the ultimate beneficiary of the trust, when it terminates, following the deaths of both the creator of the trust and the lifetime beneficiary rather than to the tax collector.

To get a better feel as to how a revocable living trust works for a married couple in California, I will recite the benefits to the client as though "you" just started the same family living trust. You be the judge of the benefits.

Case Study

Living Trust for Your Family Trust

Mr. and Mrs. Working Person,

The central document of your estate plan is your living trust. The major purpose is to effectively pass wealth from one generator to the next and so on. The living trust holds title to all of your assets, excepting, of course, those which you have transferred to the children's trust or gifted outright to your children (ten thousand dollars maximum, per person, per child, tax-free). The purpose of the transfer of your assets into a trust is to avoid a probate of the assets, and to afford you death tax savings and a plan for the disposition of the assets upon your respective deaths. Probate, with its attendant expense and delays up to two years, is eliminated because no change in title to your assets is necessary on your deaths. Title to the assets remains in the trust, and the persons entitled to succeed to the use and benefit of the assets are determined by the terms of the trust. A probate is essentially a court proceeding designed to determine to whom legal title to the property should pass when a current title-holder has died. Because your living trust will survive your deaths with legal title to your property undisturbed, probate is avoided.

Death tax savings is afforded by the trust by means of a division of your property in the occasion that one of you dies first. This division will prevent some of the assets subject to death tax upon the first's death, again being subject to tax on the death of your survivor, while, at the same time, allowing the survivor to return some beneficial rights to the use of those assets. Without the restriction on the use of those assets by the survivor, as set out in the trust, the assets would be fully subject to death tax on the survivor's death.

In regard to the disposition of your property upon your deaths, your living trust provides almost unlimited flexibility. The timing of distributions, identity of beneficiaries, size of interest allowed each beneficiary, and other factors can all be adjusted to effect your desires regarding the use of your property after you are dead. So long as you both are living, you can change any or all terms of the trust, take property out of the trust, or terminate the trust completely. After one of you dies, the trust becomes irrevocable and no longer can be modified or terminated, which insures that your desires in establishing the trust will not be defeated after your deaths.

As the trust is now designed, you can deal with your property much the same as if your property were not in trust, for so long as you both are living. The only substantial change will be that title to your property will be held by the trust, and you will sign papers dealing with title to your property by writing your names followed by the word "trustee." Upon the death of the first of you, the terms of the trust become irrevocable and nonmodifiable, and the property in the trust is divided into separate trusts, Trust A and Trust B. Trust B will contain an amount of property equal to the maximum unified credit equivalent available at the time of the first death. The unified credit is a credit against taxes that would otherwise be due on the transfer of assets by gift or device. The unified credit equivalent is simply the amount of the property that you pass without the payment of any estate or gift tax. For persons dying in 1986, the unified credit equivalent is the sum of $500,000. Under current law, the unified credit is scheduled to increase to a $600,000 maximum in 1987. Thus, for a person dying in or after 1987, the maximum amount of property that can be given away (other than to that person's spouse or certain charitable beneficiaries), without incurring gift or estate tax, is $600,000. Trust A will consist of the surviving spouse's one-half interest in the community property; his or her separate property, which has been placed into the trust; and any other trust property that is not included in Trust B.

After the first death, the survivor will have the right to withdraw up to the entire principal of Trust A. In addition, the survivor will have a limited right to withdraw the greater of $5,000 or 5 percent of the value of the trust from the principal of Trust B each year. In addition, a special trustee will be appointed with respect to Trust B. This special trustee will have the authority to determine the survivor's needs, if any, for the income from Trust B. If, in the judgment of the special trustee, the survivor needs any portion, up to the whole, or the income from Trust B for his or her support, health, maintenance, and/or education, the trustee may pay that to the survivor.

On the death of the survivor, the trust would be divided into equal shares for the benefit of your children or, if your children do not survive you, for the benefit of your grandchildren. The shares so set aside for your children would be contributed outright to them since they are now over the age of 21. With respect to the shares set aside for a grandchild who has not yet reached the age of 21, that share would remain in trust to the benefit of the grandchild until he or she attains the age of 21.

As you know, the living trust has been prepared to insure that all of your property will pass in exact accordance with your wishes. To further insure that your wishes are carried out, you have both signed "pour-over" wills. The wills provide that any property that either of you hold in your personal name at your death will, upon your death, go into and be held by your trust. The wills will affect only property that you failed to charge into the name of your trust before your death. While the wills will preserve the tax savings and depositive objective of your trust with respect to the assets passing under them the probate avoidance feature of the trust will be lost with respect to such assets. Although the California Probate Code authorized certain simplified procedures in the case of small estates that are short of a formal probate, it is nonetheless important that you are careful to change title to "all" of your assets to the name of your trust to avoid the need for formal probate of any of them under your wills.

In California, the community property agreement provides that all the property, other than insurance policies and any bank accounts in the separate name of either of you, will be community property. Community property receives very special, favorable treatment under the income tax law upon the death of a spouse having an interest in it. Upon the death of a spouse, all the community property in which he or she has an interest will have its income tax base increased to its then fair market value. This will reduce capital gains that the surviving spouse will have to pay tax upon when he or she sells a community property asset after the death of his or her spouse. Community property agreement will assure you that you will receive the favorable tax treatment, with respect to all of your property, and the unlimited marital deduction for estate tax purposes.

WHO CAN A LIVING TRUST HELP MOST?

A living trust may have seemed to you something far off and distant, something only for later. Upon reading this case study, you can identify needs that are important to your personal estate planning. Many people want to enjoy what they have earned or inherited and dislike being involved in the problems of managing capital so the co-trustee can do it.

Forward-looking individuals gain a lot of satisfaction in establishing a program to cover all contingencies for the future benefit of their family or their favorite charity.

Widows, orphans, and any other men or women with little experience in financial management, seek and need impartial and trustworthy advise from an objective, knowledgeable, yet friendly trustee.

YOUR OWN TRUST IS EASY TO START

Set your objectives so your living trust can be tailor-made to meet the needs and circumstances of you and your family. We would be happy to advise our clients on how to best attain their objectives, but only after they decide what the objectives are. Since your living trust will be a centerpiece of your immediate and future plans, an expert lawyer should draw it, with all the provisions needed to achieve your specific purposes.

THE PSYCHOLOGICAL BENEFIT OF A TRUST

As a rule, single people, young and old alike, are less likely to think of estate problems and trusts than couples are, especially those with children.

Everyone needs to provide for an old age in an era in which inflation can wipe out a lifetime's earnings within a few years, in addition to the taxes that have to be paid. Professional management can be a tremendous help in the later years.

Think, just for a brief moment, what would happen if you suffered a crippling heart attack, or debilitating disease, or had an accident or stroke that made you unconscious for a long period of time? What would happen to your affairs during that time? In many instances, when people recover, the financial chaos is more debilitating than the illness.

You need some lawful instrument in your estate, to deal with things if you become disabled and cannot look after your own affairs. There are unethical people who prey on the elderly; if you set up a trust, that shouldn't happen.

WHAT IS AN ESTATE?

Anyone who owns property or has a dollar that he or she does not plan to spend has an "estate." The state and federal government may have something to say about what he or she can do with it. But no other person can tell you what to do with that property, whether to keep it, sell it, exchange it, or give it away. No one can tell you what to do with the dollar, whether to put it into a savings account or whatever. You alone can plan your estate.

Although you may be a working person and know nothing about the technical aspects of estate planning, you are the only person competent to decide what is to be done with your estate; what risks are to be taken to build it; what security measures are to be taken to preserve it; how much you would like to have available for the education of yourself or your children; how much is available for your own retirement; who is to get what, and when they are to get it, after you are gone; and many other details.

There are value judgments to be made. There is a personal investment philosophy, an attitude toward risk. There are blood and emotional ties to be considered. No outsider can impose his values, his philosophy, his feelings on the estate owner.

But society can and does impose laws and taxes that affect whatever you might plan. Mortimer Caplin, former commissioner of the Internal Revenue, wasn't joking when he said, "There is one difference between a tax collector and a taxidermist—the taxidermist leaves the hide." My suggestion to you is that, with proper planning, the tax collector can be persuaded to spare the hide.

Trade Secret Number 68

The estate owner is the only one competent to plan his or her own estate, but he or she needs professional help.

Trade Secret Number 69

Revocable living trusts are the best way to AVOID probate and to provide convenient and private continuity of your estate.

COMMON ESTATE-BUILDING CONCERNS

1. Having a comfortable income when you retire.
2. The impact of inflation on your assets.
3. Accumulating a fund for the use of your children's education.
4. The management of your estate for your spouse and children in your absence.

5. How your life insurance proceeds will be invested and managed.
6. Provisions for your children's finances in the case of the premature death of you and your spouse.
7. How the taxes will be paid upon the estates of you and your spouse.

LIVING TRUST ESTATE-BUILDING BENEFITS

Your living trust can provide for an accumulation program for your retirement and the educational needs of your children. You can decide who receives the income and principal of your trust, when it is received, and how it will be received. Payments can be scheduled for your children in order to provide for their comfort, maintenance, support, and education. Insurance proceeds can immediately pass into a trust to assure they will be used for your family members by the trustees. A flexible investment program and flexible trust provisions can be structured to meet changing economic conditions and varying family needs. You can also save a lot of money in income and estate taxes.

RETIRED AND WIDOWED PEOPLE

Your retirement trust can provide for a check sent monthly to you or to your bank account. Your trustee can establish a professionally managed investment portfolio offering a hedge against inflation. Your trustees can pay bills for you and your dependents, in the event of illness or incapacity, and can make principal available in the event of an emergency. The trust will also provide for the passage of your assets while minimizing the cost, delay, and publicity of probate proceedings.

A HELPING HAND

Living trusts can be used to assist your children or grandchildren who are just getting started, to help provide them with a college or professional education, or simply to make them financially independent. Such trusts frequently save substantial income taxes.

CONTROL

The outstanding advantage of a revocable living trust is that you can watch it work. If experience suggests changes, you can make them. The revocable living trust may be amended at any time; you can add or delete beneficiaries, change trustees, or revoke the trust.

THE AVOIDANCE OF PROBATE

The revocable living trust need not end with your death but may continue for the benefit of other family members. Thus, neither disability nor death interrupts the preplanned investment program.

Probate is a name encompassing the proof of a will, and the judicial administration has serious drawbacks of delays, expense, and publicity. Family members often wait several years for the final distribution of an estate. Probate costs include the fees of executors, attorneys, accountants, and appraisers, plus court costs and other expenses. Estates are valued on total value, which means if you owe $80,000 on a $150,000 residence, the house is valued at $150,000 not the $70,000 equity above the mortgage.

On an estate of $200,000, probate costs average $15,400; $300,000—$22,200; and $400,000—$28,700. Because the assets in a living trust are generally not subject to probate, the trust avoids delays and expense. Moreover, the living trust avoids any publicity of the size of the estate and the identity of its beneficiaries. Probated wills are generally public records, while living trusts are private and personal. The cost for a living trust can range from $1,000 to $2,000 or can be free with certain IRA or mutual fund investments.

FINAL THOUGHT ON TRUSTS

Everyone, whether he or she realizes it or not, has in force a legal plan for the disposition of their property when they die. You determine what that plan is by choice, with a written legal document, or the law steps in and disposes of the estate in a manner that the law "assumes" you would have "intended." So, estate planning is already determined by law, unless you decide to personally make that decision for your family and heirs.

Chapter 14

THE 10-PERCENT ENTREPRENEURIAL SOLUTION

The 10 percent invested in entrepreneurial ventures can exceed the return on the 70–20 part of the investment rule in a short period of time. In the event your "entrepreneur" ventures don't work out, the diversification in the 70-percent real estate and 20-percent mutual funds will still allow you to become a millionaire.

Keep 10 percent of investment capital in liquid, guaranteed government securities, "ready" for the "right" entrepreneurial high-return opportunity. Be patient and selective, and the entreprenurial investment vehicle "you" decide to pursue may supersede all other investment vehicles in your diversified portfolio.

In the event you invest impulsively and lose the 10 percent, you still satisfied a psychological need to maximize your profits. At worst, you can save another 10 percent and try again, with more insight and experience, and later achieve the geometric high financial reward reserved in society for the "members only" club called entrepreneurs.

ENTREPRENEURIAL AWARENESS

There is no shortage of entrepreneurial opportunities. The hard thing is to become aware of them and make sure they have a feasible business plan with proper capitalization and management. Some areas of opportunity to consider include:

1. telecommunication products and services;
2. robotics;
3. biotechnology;
4. all service-oriented businesses;
5. firing the boss and going into business;
6. being a silent partner in corporate buy-outs;
7. venture capital (investing in or finding special situations);
8. going to work for an entrepreneur;
9. investing with "rising star" entrepreneurs;
10. oil and gas;
11. strategic metals;
12. land assemblage;
13. research and development projects;
14. art, gold, silver, collectibles;
15. new issues.

HUMAN NATURE

It is worth 10 percent of your money to satisfy the psychological need to think big. You don't have to settle for a lottery ticket to rationalize your entrepreneurial cravings, or wait for the boss at work to get promoted or die. You can move forward in tempo with your talents, experience, and guts by selecting an active or passive entrepreneurial investment vehicle. The entrepreneur never has to wait for other circumstances beyond reason or control to move ahead. The entrepreneur finds a need and provides a profitable service.

VENTURE CAPITAL

Almost all venture capital investments have come from conservative institutions such as banks, insurance companies, pension funds, and wealthy families. Venture capital sources in 1984 were:

6 percent—corporations;
13 percent—endowments and foundations;
14 percent—insurance companies;
15 percent—wealthy individuals and families;
18 percent—foreign investors;
34 percent—pension funds.

There are now investment vehicles that allow individuals to participate in diversified and single-venture capital projects for as little as $5,000. These partnerships strive to earn at least 30 percent a year, compounded over the life of the project under conditions of managed risk. These venture capital groups usually invest in 15–30 companies with commercial products and/or services that "expert management" believes to have potential for superior growth, making an initial public offering within eighteen months to three years after the investment. Returns on selected venture capital investment have run as high as 500,000 percent, which means that a few good selections more than balance the losses and risk, as part of your overall diversified portfolio. This extremely favorable risk-reward ratio is what has attracted conservative, risk-adverse institutions like banks, insurance companies, and pension funds to venture capital. It is hard to pick all outright losers to invest in, and even losers have some value. And just a couple of winners cover all the portfolio's bad bets. Remember, entrepreneurial investments are often high risk, so limit yourself to 10 percent of capital investments, which is the most you are willing to risk and possibly lose.

IT ALL DEPENDS

An entrepreneurial situation can be high risk–high return, high risk–low return, high risk–no return, and low risk–high return. It all depends on what you are trying to do, the help you have, how you structure and package, and the timing of the entrepreneurial venture. What I am trying to say is that "the risk" can be shared, restricted, avoided, or even shifted upon the happening or nonhappening of specified contingencies. I believe in small deals, medium-size, and large ventures. What's important is that you have someone else involved who can improve the chances of success, and always base your assumptions on "conversative" feasibility projections. You want to have ways to control the risk and reduce risk as well as contingency plans, in the event you have to modify, change, or abandon the business plan.

In my own financial planning practice, I spend most of my time researching and finding select investment vehicles for my clients. I practice the 70–20–10 investment rule with the same concerns to maximize investment profits in relation to the risk with proper diversification.

Problem solving, consulting, and structuring entrepreneurial ventures improves the investment result. My challenge is to structure and package the investment vehicle to meet the specific client's personal situation. We strive to create a competitive advantage with "contingency" plans, in the event the client's situation changes. The only purpose of investing is to increase your net worth in a diversified manner in concert with your overall objectives.

INVESTMENT VERSUS SPECULATION

It is often difficult to draw a sharp distinction between investment and speculation. However, a few skillful changes in the structure, capitalization, service, product, economy, or management can drastically effect the final outcome. The only purpose of investing is to gain the maximum return for the risk you are willing to take. The entrepreneur always has methods to reduce the speculative risk.

BALANCE THE RISKS

The working person needs risk-management insurance to provide for both personal and business bad contingencies; access to adequate emergency funds for your life-style; and the 70–20–10 investment rule to provide for a balanced, diversified portfolio. The complete financial planning package, including a living trust, should be custom designed to flexibly meet your changing personal situation.

In essence, the entrepreneurial venture should be structured to provide a "superior" profit and not be labeled 100-percent pure speculation. For example, driving a car is a good investment, especially if it takes you to and from the place you make money. If your car needs adjustments for repairs, accidents, and so on, you press on because of the overall convenience and benefits of "driving." If you drive your car "blindfolded" to work, it will become the most costly, tragic, and speculative venture you ever tried. You might not even have the privilege to recover or recall making it.

You do have 100-percent control of your thoughts. You also have the insight to reduce the entrepreneurial risk from your point of view and still achieve a tremendous profit incentive. In the event that the risk far outweighs the reward and your control of the situation, leave your money in liquid, government securities. Later, you will find the right, feasible entrepreneurial venture to accomplish your high-profit objective.

THE VALUE OF YOUR SIGNATURE

You have something close to you that will yield a large profit. Let your subconscious mind reveal it to you.

One of the most profitable, safe, entrepreneurial investments ever made by a major corporation was when one person had the initiative to lease, long-term, for nine dollars a square foot, several floors in the World Trade Center. Today's market rental cost per square foot is thirty-four dollars and going up.

"Your" signature on a contract as coordinator, representative of someone or something, exclusive agent for persons or services, on a master lease, on a long-term option, and many other things, can create exponential entrepreneurial returns, with no money down, just by making intelligent business decisions.

THE CHALLENGE

"The greatest innovations for new jobs, technologies, and economic vigor today come from a small but growing circle of heroes, the small business people, American entrepreneurs, the men and women of faith, intellect, and daring who take great risks to invest in and invent our future."

Ronald Reagan
President of the United States
May, 1985

Trade Secret Number 70
Your ideas will produce entrepreneurial results.

Chapter 15

THE DAY AFTER

The day after you realize that you are a millionaire, you will feel nostalgic and will recall the friends and the good and bad decisions that you encountered along the way.

You have accomplished an American Dream, to stockpile a lot of money through your own initiative. You will now understand and appreciate why the wealthy strive to preserve and increase their financial fortune.

Living off the interest earned on your investment portfolio will govern your new life-style. You will develop new challenges in life and will always strive to inflation-index and to preserve your wealth. Your investment portfolio will seek a safe, realistic rate of return. A net profit, after taxes and inflation, is the only way to preserve purchasing power.

FOR THE REST OF YOUR LIFE

For the rest of your life you will always realize that:

1. Everything that you create begins in the form of a thought.
2. New goals are always set to meet changing needs.
3. Definiteness of purpose will lead to progress.
4. The services of expert professional advisors is necessary for survival.
5. The habit of saving 10 percent or more of earnings makes dreams become reality.

6. The Individual Retirement Account (IRA) is the most sensible investment vehicle to take advantage of favorable tax treatment when planning for future security.
7. The 70–20–10 investment rule can make people multimillionaires.
8. The purpose of all investments is to improve one's net worth, and the annual review of the financial balance sheet measures the exact performance to date.
9. All people naturally desire knowledge, and giving more of yourself is always a rewarding experience.
10. The main event in life is sharing ideas and helping other people.

Peace, prosperity, tolerance, persistence, love, and health are choices. Let us make these choices once again for ourselves, our friends, and for mankind.

Trade Secret Number 71
The next thought is fully under your control.

LOUIS F. PETROSSI, C.F.P.

Mr. Petrossi conducts money-making financial seminars and offers personal financial planning services internationally. Services offered include:

1. Flexible financial planning strategies for individuals;
2. The best way to manage IRA and pension funds;
3. How to evaluate investments;
4. Financial planning for corporate personnel;
5. Creative real estate techniques;
6. Estate planning concepts;
7. The extra profits in joint ventures;
8. How to improve cash flow and reduce taxes;
9. Women's financial independence programs;
10. Conventions.

Louis F. Petrossi is a problem-solver and knows how to improve the investment results of almost any situation he encounters.

Imagination is far more important than knowledge, but good ideas and plans must be implemented to assure successful results. In the event you would like Louis F. Petrossi's personal assistance, please feel free to write the letter on page 130.

Dear Lou:

I need your help with the following:

- ☐ A financial plan
- ☐ Tax-free income recommendations
- ☐ Professional money management
- ☐ Retirement planning
- ☐ Diversified tax reform favored investments
- ☐ Structuring my pension plan to yield 21% annually
- ☐ Keynote speaker

Name ______________________________

Address ______________ City ______________

State ______________ Zip code ______________

Phone (   ) ______________

Mail to: Louis F. Petrossi
P.O. Box 6097
McLean VA 22106